Contemporary Issues in Sports Economics

NEW HORIZONS IN THE ECONOMICS OF SPORT

Series Editors: Wladimir Andreff, *Department of Economics, University of Paris 1 Panthéon Sorbonne, France* and Marc Lavoie, *Department of Economics, University of Ottawa, Canada*

For decades, the economics of sport was regarded as a hobby for a handful of professional economists who were primarily involved in other areas of research. In recent years, however, the significance of the sports economy as a percentage of GDP has expanded dramatically. This has coincided with an equivalent rise in the volume of economic literature devoted to the study of sport.

This series provides a vehicle for deeper analyses of the demand for sport, cost–benefit analysis of sport, sporting governance, the economics of professional sports and leagues, individual sports, trade in the sporting goods industry, media coverage, sponsoring and numerous related issues. It contributes to the further development of sports economics by welcoming new approaches and highlighting original research in both established and newly emerging sporting activities. The series publishes the best theoretical and empirical work from well-established researchers and academics, as well as from talented newcomers in the field.

Titles in the series include:

The Economics of Sport and the Media
Edited by Claude Jeanrenaud and Stefan Késenne

The Economic Theory of Professional Team Sports
An Analytical Treatment
Stefan Késenne

Economics, Uncertainty and European Football
Trends in Competitive Balance
Loek Groot

The Political Economy of Professional Sport
Jean-François Bourg and Jean-Jacques Gouguet

Contemporary Issues in Sports Economics
Participation and Professional Team Sports
Edited by Wladimir Andreff

Contemporary Issues in Sports Economics

Participation and Professional Team Sports

Edited by

Wladimir Andreff

Professor Emeritus, Department of Economics, University of Paris 1 Panthéon Sorbonne, France

NEW HORIZONS IN THE ECONOMICS OF SPORTS

Edward Elgar

Cheltenham, UK • Northampton, MA, USA

Published by
Edward Elgar Publishing Limited
The Lypiatts
15 Lansdown Road
Cheltenham
Glos GL50 2JA
UK

Edward Elgar Publishing, Inc.
William Pratt House
9 Dewey Court
Northampton
Massachusetts 01060
USA

A catalogue record for this book
is available from the British Library

Library of Congress Control Number: 2010929042

MIX
Paper from
responsible sources
FSC® C018575
FSC
www.fsc.org

ISBN 978 1 84980 447 9

Typeset by Servis Filmsetting Ltd, Stockport, Cheshire
Printed and bound by MPG Books Group, UK

Contents

Figures

Tables

Contributors

Wladimir Andreff, University Paris 1 Panthéon Sorbonne, Centre d'Economie de la Sorbonne, France, Honorary President of the International Association of Sport Economists.

Markus Breuer, Institute of Sport Science, School of Social and Behavioral Sciences, Friedrich-Schiller-University Jena, Germany.

Raul Caruso, Institute of Economic Policy, Catholic University of the Sacred Heart, Milan, Italy.

Frank Daumann, Institute of Sport Science, School of Social and Behavioral Sciences, Friedrich-Schiller-University Jena, Germany.

Peter Dawson, Department of Economics, University of Bath, UK.

Paul Downward, Institute of Sport and Leisure Policy, Loughborough University, UK.

Jaume García, Department of Economics and Business, Universitat Pompeu Fabra, Barcelona, Spain.

Joel G. Maxcy, University of Georgia, Athens, Georgia, USA.

Levi Pérez, Department of Economics, University of Oviedo, Fundación Observatorio Económico del Deporte, Oviedo, Spain.

Gaël Raballand, World Bank, Washington, PhD in Economics from the University Paris 1 Panthéon Sorbonne, France.

Plácido Rodríguez, Department of Economics, University of Oviedo, Director of Fundación Observatorio Económico del Deporte, Oviedo, Spain.

Stefan Szymanski, Cass Business School, London, UK.

Acknowledgements

This volume contains a set of original essays written by eminent European – and one eminent American – sports economists. The aim of the volume is to present recent research results in contemporary sports economics, with a focus on sport participation and professional team sports, and to analyse developments, prospects and key policy concerns related to these issues. The draft versions of the chapters were originally presented at the First European Conference in Sports Economics held in the economic research centre (Centre d'Economie de la Sorbonne) of the University Paris 1 Panthéon Sorbonne (France) in September 2009. The Conference was organized by Wladimir Andreff and hosted at the Maison des Sciences Economiques of the University Paris 1.

I would like to express my special gratitude for their financial or technical support to the University Paris 1 Panthéon Sorbonne, the Centre d'Economie de la Sorbonne, the UEFA and the Sport Unit of the European Commission. The Conference would not have been a success without a heavy personal investment by Madeleine Andreff, Charlotte Cabane, Marie-José Desaigues, Barbara Despiney, Waldemar Karpa and Sandrine Poupaux, and I was surrounded warmly by this very efficient organizing committee for months. I would finally thank all those who have agreed to act as peer reviewers of the papers submitted to the Conference and then to this volume. I am also grateful to those who chaired the different sessions or delivered keynote speeches at the Conference.

1. Contemporary issues in sports economics: a selection

Wladimir Andreff

INTRODUCTION

Sports economics has developed rapidly during the past ten years. The number of contemporary issues has skyrocketed. Though the first paper published dates back to Rottenberg (1956), sports economics is only now really considered to be an established academic discipline. Sports economists' common knowledge has been gathered into a handbook (Andreff and Szymanski, 2006), while two double volumes have collected the most representative papers published before the beginning of the previous and the current decade (Zimbalist, 2001; Andreff, forthcoming). Two new scientific journals[1] entirely dedicated to sports economics have opened a wide path to article publication on both well-known and breaking issues. Finally, the 2000s are characterised by the emergence of textbooks on both sides of the Atlantic – the North American (Leeds and von Allmen, 2002; Fort, 2003; Sandy, Sloane and Rosentraub, 2004) and the European with Downward, Dawson and Dejonghe (2009), as well as a more theoretical piece by Késenne (2007).

In this context, contemporary issues in sports economics are so numerous that each conference or book has to cover some tightly focused topics. There were eight of them at the first European Conference in Sports Economics held in Paris in September 2009: the economics of professional team sports leagues; the economic dimensions of sport participation; sport financing and governance; professional sports markets; the economic impact of sport mega-events; the labour market in professional sports; measuring sport efficiency; and regulation and competitive balance in professional sports leagues. However, given the larger number of papers presented on professional team sports, it was predictable that enough

1

of them would rank among the best and the selection process would produce yet another book simply on professional sports. This is not exactly what materialised. First, because the economics of sport participation is to some extent unheeded in the sports economics literature and excellent papers have tackled connected issues at the aforementioned European conference, two of them form the first part of this book. Secondly, those issues which are the most examined in the literature on professional team sports are competitive balance, competition and regulation in team sports leagues, labour markets for talent, and sports events and their economic impact. As it happens, screening the best papers on a peer-review basis resulted in a selection of chapters for this book which are geared towards issues that are less investigated so far in the usual literature on professional team sports, such as: sport financing and governance, sport betting, and the impact of low scoring on competitive balance and fan attractiveness in European football. Just one chapter tackles more traditional issues with regard to luxury tax, payrolls and player transfers in baseball, though it provides new insights. All the rest of this volume strays from the beaten track. The reader could not find similar topics in the above-mentioned handbook and textbooks, or most specialised journals.

The first part of the volume is devoted to the economic analysis of sport participation determinants and social impact, whereas the second part is about less-investigated issues in the economics of professional team sports. In some sense, each part stands on one of the two extreme edges of sports economics.

ECONOMIC ANALYSIS OF SPORT PARTICIPATION DETERMINANTS AND SOCIAL IMPACT

The economics of sport participation for all in grassroots sports is still in its infancy since it attracts little money per sport participant, which is sometimes an excuse to contend that there is no room for sound economic analysis. This volume provides some evidence that such a view is misleading. On the one hand, there are a number of economic determinants to grassroots sport participation; such as: whether access to the sport is free or requires an entrance fee in the commercial sport sector; the level of the sport participants' income;

ssroots than professional sports finance.[2] When it comes to the
ancing of professional team sports, an analysis has demonstrated
ort of convergence between European and North American major
orts toward a common contemporary model of finance relying,
t of all, on TV rights revenues, then new sources of finance such
merchandising, corporate finance, trading players and the stock
hange (Andreff and Staudohar, 2000). However, such a model
not prevented European football from sinking into a deep finan-
l crisis.[3]

On the other hand, the issue of governance in professional sports
gues has recently been tackled; namely, a link has been estab-
ied between the weak quality of the governance in professional
orts clubs and their financial deficits, through the concept of a
b's soft budget constraint – and the real practice of clubs' bail-
s in an econometrically verified vicious circle between the TV
send and salary inflation (Andreff, 2007b).

n Chapter 4, Stefan Szymanski broadens the analysis to both
fessional and grassroots sports taken together, starting from
voluntary nature of much sporting activity, recognised in the
oon treaty. This recognises the reality that most European sport
ot organised on commercial lines; it has to rely on state funding.
h reality sometimes clashes with a small number of clubs and
e players who generate large incomes and demand a significant
over the way that their sport is run. Relying on such a dividing
, Szymanski's analysis identifies two current financial crises in
opean sports, one concerning professional sports such as foot-
, the other hitting local grassroots sports clubs. In the first case,
os overspend on player talents in the pursuit of success, putting
nselves in financial jeopardy: around 50 English football clubs
e entered into administration. Even those European leagues
re football clubs have tighter financial regulation have not
ped financial crisis. On the other hand, grassroots sports clubs
in crisis because it has become harder to obtain public subsidies,
to fiscal deficit, and membership and volunteerism are under
sure.

hen the governance issue comes to the fore. Professional clubs
t a bigger say in the running of national federations, to reflect
significance of their financial contributions, and their wealthy
powerful owners have little reverence for national traditions
port, while in some countries the government steps in to fill

transportation costs to the sport facility; and subsidies by local
authorities and the government to back the development of sport
for all. This book shows that the list must be extended to include
social determinants, namely household attitudes or habits regarding watching sports on TV, that may impact on sport participation.
Moreover it demonstrates that studying the relationships between
sport participation and sport viewing can be empirically analysed
and verified with the usual economic and econometric methodology.
The same comment applies to the study of the relationship between
crime and sport participation. It is easy to guess that the social
impact of sport participation on criminality is rather complex, but
an economic approach to the whole issue helps to delineate the sorts
of crime on which sport participation really has an alleviating effect.

It was suggested long ago that viewing live sports events or watching them on TV should trigger an increased participation in the sport
disciplines which are more easily accessible to fans or TV viewers;
thus disparities between different sport disciplines will be exacerbated by uneven stadium and media exposure (Andreff, 1981). Often
assumed, but never empirically tested, this assumption has remained
implicit so far. Chapter 2, by Peter Dawson and Paul Downward,
analyses official data about sport participation in the UK using an
econometric model to check whether sports participation and sports
spectatorship are systematically linked. Despite UK policy priorities
that include increasing participation in sport and physical activity as
a precondition for health and success in international competition,
there has been little work on possible relationships between sports
participation and event spectatorship. Such a relationship is all the
more likely in that many grassroots sport participants are consumers of live or media sport events, but it has been almost completely
ignored in the literature.

In economic terms, this means that we do not know yet whether
there is a substitutionary or complementary relationship between the
demands for sports participation, sports live attendance and televised
sports. Dawson and Downward fill this gap by using a zero-inflated
count model tested with standard OLS methodology, and then test
this further with Poisson and negative binomial models (with a logit
specification in the latter case). Various tests confirm that the zero-
inflated negative binomial model is the best performing. The results
regarding the variables of interest show that watching TV sports has
a positive and significant effect on sports participation but attending

one or more live sporting event during the previous four weeks has the largest impact on sports participation. Whilst TV in general is a substitute for sports participation, televised sport is a complement. A complementary relationship between sports participation and viewing sports either live or via the media is validated. This result supports the current emphasis of sports policy in the UK, particularly in the case of the Olympic Games, which assumes that attending live sport or watching TV sport might encourage participation. Other variables included on the right-hand side of the tested models indicate that being male, younger, unmarried and broadly white British promotes sports participation, as does education, whereas the presence of children in the household and smoking both reduce participation.

A widespread view holds that sport is beneficial for society; this is a common assumption underlying both the UK's and other European countries' sports policies and a recent White Paper issued by the European Commission. The contention is that sport participation is good for health, hinders obesity and reduces health expenditures, contributes to the (physical) education of the population, favours social integration of minorities, develops fighting spirit or at least competitive spirit, teaches co-operation within a team, and increases the wage and labour outcomes of sport participants compared to non-participants. However, the question whether sport could have a social benefit in preventing crime has not been dealt with so far. No clear relationship has been established between sport participation and crime, but if it did result in reduced criminal activity, spending on sport might enable a reduction in the amount of money invested in crime prevention and sanctions.

Raul Caruso (Chapter 3) takes the opportunity of using existing data about Italian regions to approach the aforementioned relationship under the assumption that a social outcome exhibiting fewer crimes must be preferred to one characterised by a higher level of crime. Thus, from the very beginning, the impact of sport participation on crime is expected to be negative – that is, to reduce criminality. Caruso interprets sport participation as a good exhibiting a multiple nature that combines exchange, coercion and integrative relationships in accordance with Kenneth Boulding's theoretical approach to a social system. This is completed using an emerging theory of relational goods which perfectly fits with Boulding's approach of integrative systems. Relational goods are produced

through social interactions among individuals, ar their production and consumption cannot be dis end of the day, a relational good is nothing but itself. From this, Caruso derives a conjecture statir be socially beneficial as long as relational behaviou coercive and exchange components.

The above-mentioned conjecture is then er through the relationship between sport participatio of crime: property crime (thefts, robberies and bu crime (rapes, homicides, kidnappings, injuries and nile crime (every crime committed by young peopl 18). The results show that sport participation sig the level of property crime, is positively but weakl violent crime, and is negatively related to juvenile an interaction between sport participation and ed ited and can be explained in line with psychologi participation may be an incubator for developi abilities which reinforce cognitive abilities provid attainment. Thus, sport participation can hinder p nile crime but it may trigger some violent crime.

THE ECONOMICS OF PROFESSIONA SPORTS

In this volume I have avoided those issues on wl professional team sports has been elaborated agai years, that is competitive balance, the objective fu league regulation (rookie draft, salary cap, reve across the member teams) versus competition po would hope to develop a wider understanding of p and move on to consider issues that have been ig investigated less.

Sport financing, be it for grassroots or profes long way from being the most investigated issue ics. In the case of European sports, some breaktl achieved regarding overall sports finance in 12 tries due to a Council of Europe initiative (Ani An update has been provided recently covering Union members (Amnyos, 2008) which offers m

the income gap between professional and grassroots sports. Thus Szymanski contends that the state is 'the elephant in the room' in a pyramidal European model of sport. Sports federations tend to see government as a source of finance, but resist the attempts of government to impose its priorities, whereas governments tend to consider federations as fully representative of all sport, thus neglecting the role of both business and autonomous self-organised (by the participants) sports. In conclusion, the chapter presents a matrix model of European sport which is more likely to capture the roots of its current crisis.

While in European sport systems, taxation and revenue redistribution in the form of subsidies from the richest professional sports are basically public, as Szymanski argues, in North American sports, a 'private' taxation and revenue distribution is confined to intra-league mechanisms. One case in point is the so-called luxury tax applied to the highest spending teams in a league when their payroll is in excess of a defined threshold. Joel Maxcy reminds us that the 1997 collective bargaining agreement between the Major League Baseball (MLB) owners and the players' union introduced a luxury tax on club payrolls, renamed the competitive balance tax since 2006, for the purpose of enhancing competitive balance (Chapter 5). From his theoretical model, Maxcy concludes that a luxury tax reduces the incentive to hire talent beyond the tax threshold. Then an empirical model of player transfers in the context of a luxury tax is developed and tested with MLB data, since changes in the distribution of talent can be evidenced in detail by player mobility across clubs. Contrary to popular wisdom, the results provide general support for the effectiveness of the luxury tax in restraining spending by high revenue teams.

Another follow-up to Szymanski's chapter is that a new source of money is flowing into sport at a skyrocketing pace: betting and gambling on sporting outcomes. However, it is not without its problem since one single sport betting company is (or was, as in Germany) a public monopoly in various European countries in order to prevent people from developing a pathological gambling addiction. On the other hand, levying a percentage on the public betting company's sales is an easy channel for transferring some monies to the government sports budget or, as in France, to some para-fiscal fund that supplements a tiny sports budget. Such a channel is used to finance grassroots sports, but now the sport betting industry has to be open to competition in compliance with EU deregulation. A threat is felt by all in the sport movement, basically at grassroots level, while sport betting in Europe will become a fully-fledged market activity in the near future.

Frank Daumann and Markus Breuer (Chapter 6) use the sport betting markets – where information is processed by bookmakers to enhance forecasts about sporting outcomes – for testing market efficiency. Information is differentiated into three subsets: information known before the season (long-term performance of a team), information influencing the winning probability and becoming obvious during a match (which cannot be used to forecast winning probabilities), and relevant information which becomes public during the current season (dependent on time). Postulating an efficient utilisation of available information, Daumann and Breuer ask whether the quality of the forecasts would improve during a sport season. Calculating win probabilities, they find some surprising results. Bookmaker forecasts are not better than those obtained only by chance. The assumption of an increasing quality of forecasting over the sport season is not verified. However such conclusions cannot be generalised due to the limited size of the matchday sample. One of the rather provocative implications derived by the authors is that a football match outcome may well depend on chance to a large extent. This challenges the current view that a team performance is closely linked to its financial possibilities, if not in the long run, at least on a matchday or even during a season.

Football pools in the gambling market in Spain are also used as a new source of revenue for the government to further promote sporting activities. Revenues from football pools channel significant investment into football-related social causes. Since revenues are a fixed proportion of sales, Jaume García, Levi Pérez and Plácido Rodríguez (Chapter 7) investigate whether football pools managers adopt a revenue-maximising objective in looking at the determinants of participation such as price, the size of the prize pool and the difficulty of the game. The composition of betting coupons, in terms of teams included, is also taken into account. Two modes of betting can be offered to the bettors: the effective price model and the jackpot model. This may influence the demand for football pools in Spain, the determinants of which are analysed in this chapter. The jackpot from one fixture to the next one induces variation in the top prize as well as in the expected return. The composition of betting coupons is expected to affect participation strongly, the expectation being that the teams included in each bet represent a decisive determinant of participation and act as a key variable of football pools management.

The major results drawn from an OLS estimation of both effective price and jackpot models with instrumental variables show that individuals betting on the exact score are more loyal and skilled bettors than those just guessing which team wins. For both games (score or win betting), the jackpot model fits the data better than the effective price model. Considering long-run price elasticity of sales, *El Quinigol* (score betting) implies revenue maximisation while *La Quiniela* (win betting) could increase its revenues by changing the game design. In the short term, bets in *El Quinigol* are quite sensitive to changes in the effective price instead of increases in the jackpot. Not including First Division teams in the betting coupon has a relatively important (negative) impact on sales for win betting but a quite small effect on sales for score betting.

In the final chapter, Wladimir Andreff and Gaël Raballand start from the evidence of an increasing percentage of games resulting in a 0–0 draw or a 1–0 win in the five major European football leagues. They first check that any explanation of such a trend cannot be found in the literature about competitive balance and game attendance (and find very few references), while both may be affected by the trend towards low scoring on the pitch. Then they gather theoretical evidence, relying on Groot's work (2008), and empirical evidence showing that lower goal scoring has slowed down competitive balance deterioration in European football. The low goal scoring trend in European football appears to be an historical one since it is triggered by increasingly defensive tactics on the pitch over many decades. Such a trend has not been countervailed by a change in FIFA rules (three points for a win), expected to produce more goals per game, fewer draws, and on top of this, more exciting games that attract more interest. Some theoretical reasons why such a measure has been counterproductive – or at least ineffective – are surveyed, together with blurred evidence derived from econometric testing so far.

Then a regression analysis is run on data on the five major European football leagues in order to check whether competitive balance is determined by goal scoring variables whilst controlling for defensive–attacking tactics, and specific league and year variables.

This inception study on a new topic exhibits the following preliminary results: team standing is improved by its defensive tactics, is negatively affected by 0–0 draws and is positively affected by 1–0 wins, but the effect of low goal scoring and defensive tactics on competitive balance is more significant in some leagues (like the French *Ligue 1*) than others, such as the German *Bundesliga*. Avenues for further research are suggested to test whether there is a trade-off for a league between attracting attendance with an improved competitive balance and scoring attractiveness, since competitive balance improves with growing 0–0 and 1–0 scores.

NOTES

1. The *Journal of Sports Economics* (since 2000) and the *International Journal of Sport Finance* (since 2006) provide two new publication options. Before 2000, economists had little opportunity to publish in the area of sports economics in either general economic journals or sport management journals; just one, the *European Journal of Sport Management*, was open to economic articles. It was established in 1992, and in 2001 became the *European Sport Management Quarterly*.
2. A summarised version of this study with an update regarding the impact of the current global financial crisis on sports finance was presented at a WEAI conference (Andreff, 2009).
3. See the special issue of the *Journal of Sports Economics* (vol. 7, no. 1, 2006) and a follow-up in vol. 8, no. 6, 2007, including Andreff (2007a).

REFERENCES

Amnyos (2008), *Etude du financement public et privé du sport*, State Secretary for Sports, Paris, October.
Andreff, W. (1981), 'Les inégalités entre les disciplines sportives: une approche économique', in C. Pociello (ed.), *Sports et société*, Paris: Vigot, 139–51.
Andreff, W. (2007a), 'French Football: A Financial Crisis Rooted in Weak Governance', *Journal of Sports Economics*, **8**, 652–61.
Andreff, W. (2007b), 'Governance Issues in French Professional Football', in P. Rodriguez, S. Késenne and J. Garcia (eds), *Governance and Competition in Professional Sports Leagues*, Oviedo: Ediciones de la Universidad de Oviedo, 55–86.
Andreff, W. (2009), 'Public and Private Financing of Sport in Europe: The Impact of Global Crisis', paper presented at the *84th Annual Conference of Western Economic Association International*, Vancouver, 29 June–3 July.

Andreff, W. (forthcoming) (ed.), *Recent Development in Sports Economics*, Cheltenham: Edward Elgar.
Andreff, W., Bourg, J.-F., Halba, B. and Nys, J.-F. (1994), 'The Economic Importance of Sport in Europe: Financing and Economic Impact', Background document to the *14th Informal Meeting of European Sports Ministers*, Council of Europe, Strasbourg, April.
Andreff, W. and Staudohar, P. (2000), 'The Evolving European Model of Professional Sports Finance', *Journal of Sports Economics*, **1** (3), 257–76.
Andreff, W. and Szymanski, S. (2006) (eds), *Handbook on the Economics of Sport*, Cheltenham: Edward Elgar.
Downward, P., Dawson, A. and Dejonghe, T. (2009), *Sports Economics: Theory, Evidence and Policy*, London: Butterworth-Heinemann.
Fort, R. (2003), *Sports Economics*, Upper Saddle River, NJ: Prentice Hall.
Groot, L. (2008), *Economics, Uncertainty and European Football: Trends in Competitive Balance*, Cheltenham: Edward Elgar.
Késenne, S. (2007), *The Economic Theory of Professional Team Sports: An Analytical Treatment*, Cheltenham: Edward Elgar.
Leeds, M. and von Allmen, P. (2002), *The Economics of Sports*, Boston, MA: Addison Wesley.
Rottenberg, S. (1956), 'The Baseball Players' Labor Market', *Journal of Political Economy*, **64**, 242–58.
Sandy, R., Sloane, P.J. and Rosentraub, M.S. (2004), *The Economics of Sport: An International Perspective*, Basingstoke: Palgrave Macmillan.
Zimbalist, A. (2001) (ed.), *The Economics of Sport*, Cheltenham: Edward Elgar.

PART I
Economic analysis of sport participation
determinants and social impact

transportation costs to the sport facility; and subsidies by local authorities and the government to back the development of sport for all. This book shows that the list must be extended to include social determinants, namely household attitudes or habits regarding watching sports on TV, that may impact on sport participation. Moreover it demonstrates that studying the relationships between sport participation and sport viewing can be empirically analysed and verified with the usual economic and econometric methodology. The same comment applies to the study of the relationship between crime and sport participation. It is easy to guess that the social impact of sport participation on criminality is rather complex, but an economic approach to the whole issue helps to delineate the sorts of crime on which sport participation really has an alleviating effect.

It was suggested long ago that viewing live sports events or watching them on TV should trigger an increased participation in the sport disciplines which are more easily accessible to fans or TV viewers; thus disparities between different sport disciplines will be exacerbated by uneven stadium and media exposure (Andreff, 1981). Often assumed, but never empirically tested, this assumption has remained implicit so far. Chapter 2, by Peter Dawson and Paul Downward, analyses official data about sport participation in the UK using an econometric model to check whether sports participation and sports spectatorship are systematically linked. Despite UK policy priorities that include increasing participation in sport and physical activity as a precondition for health and success in international competition, there has been little work on possible relationships between sports participation and event spectatorship. Such a relationship is all the more likely in that many grassroots sport participants are consumers of live or media sport events, but it has been almost completely ignored in the literature.

In economic terms, this means that we do not know yet whether there is a substitutionary or complementary relationship between the demands for sports participation, sports live attendance and televised sports. Dawson and Downward fill this gap by using a zero-inflated count model tested with standard OLS methodology, and then test this further with Poisson and negative binomial models (with a logit specification in the latter case). Various tests confirm that the zero-inflated negative binomial model is the best performing. The results regarding the variables of interest show that watching TV sports has a positive and significant effect on sports participation but attending one or more live sporting event during the previous four weeks has the largest impact on sports participation. Whilst TV in general is a substitute for sports participation, televised sport is a complement. A complementary relationship between sports participation and viewing sports either live or via the media is validated. This result supports the current emphasis of sports policy in the UK, particularly in the case of the Olympic Games, which assumes that attending live sport or watching TV sport might encourage participation. Other variables included on the right-hand side of the tested models indicate that being male, younger, unmarried and broadly white British promotes sports participation, as does education, whereas the presence of children in the household and smoking both reduce participation.

A widespread view holds that sport is beneficial for society; this is a common assumption underlying both the UK's and other European countries' sports policies and a recent White Paper issued by the European Commission. The contention is that sport participation is good for health, hinders obesity and reduces health expenditures, contributes to the (physical) education of the population, favours social integration of minorities, develops fighting spirit or at least competitive spirit, teaches co-operation within a team, and increases the wage and labour outcomes of sport participants compared to non-participants. However, the question whether sport could have a social benefit in preventing crime has not been dealt with so far. No clear relationship has been established between sport participation and crime, but if it did result in reduced criminal activity, spending on sport might enable a reduction in the amount of money invested in crime prevention and sanctions.

Raul Caruso (Chapter 3) takes the opportunity of using existing data about Italian regions to approach the aforementioned relationship under the assumption that a social outcome exhibiting fewer crimes must be preferred to one characterised by a higher level of crime. Thus, from the very beginning, the impact of sport participation on crime is expected to be negative – that is, to reduce criminality. Caruso interprets sport participation as a good exhibiting a multiple nature that combines exchange, coercion and integrative relationships in accordance with Kenneth Boulding's theoretical approach to a social system. This is completed using an emerging theory of relational goods which perfectly fits with Boulding's approach of integrative systems. Relational goods are produced through social interactions among individuals, are non-rival, and their production and consumption cannot be disentangled; at the end of the day, a relational good is nothing but the relationship itself. From this, Caruso derives a conjecture stating that sport may be socially beneficial as long as relational behaviours dominate both coercive and exchange components.

The above-mentioned conjecture is then empirically tested through the relationship between sport participation and three types of crime: property crime (thefts, robberies and burglaries), violent crime (rapes, homicides, kidnappings, injuries and lesions) and juvenile crime (every crime committed by young people below the age of 18). The results show that sport participation significantly reduces the level of property crime, is positively but weakly associated with violent crime, and is negatively related to juvenile crime. Moreover, an interaction between sport participation and education is exhibited and can be explained in line with psychological studies: sport participation may be an incubator for developing non-cognitive abilities which reinforce cognitive abilities provided by educational attainment. Thus, sport participation can hinder property and juvenile crime but it may trigger some violent crime.

THE ECONOMICS OF PROFESSIONAL TEAM SPORTS

In this volume I have avoided those issues on which the theory of professional team sports has been elaborated again and again for 50 years, that is competitive balance, the objective function of a team, league regulation (rookie draft, salary cap, revenue redistribution across the member teams) versus competition policy, and so on. I would hope to develop a wider understanding of professional sports and move on to consider issues that have been ignored or, at least, investigated less.

Sport financing, be it for grassroots or professional sports, is a long way from being the most investigated issue in sports economics. In the case of European sports, some breakthroughs have been achieved regarding overall sports finance in 12 European countries due to a Council of Europe initiative (Andreff *et al.*, 1994). An update has been provided recently covering the 27 European Union members (Amnyos, 2008) which offers more insights about grassroots than professional sports finance.[2] When it comes to the financing of professional team sports, an analysis has demonstrated a sort of convergence between European and North American major sports toward a common contemporary model of finance relying, first of all, on TV rights revenues, then new sources of finance such as merchandising, corporate finance, trading players and the stock exchange (Andreff and Staudohar, 2000). However, such a model has not prevented European football from sinking into a deep financial crisis.[3]

On the other hand, the issue of governance in professional sports leagues has recently been tackled; namely, a link has been established between the weak quality of the governance in professional sports clubs and their financial deficits, through the concept of a club's soft budget constraint – and the real practice of clubs' bailouts in an econometrically verified vicious circle between the TV godsend and salary inflation (Andreff, 2007b).

In Chapter 4, Stefan Szymanski broadens the analysis to both professional and grassroots sports taken together, starting from the voluntary nature of much sporting activity, recognised in the Lisbon treaty. This recognises the reality that most European sport is not organised on commercial lines; it has to rely on state funding. Such reality sometimes clashes with a small number of clubs and elite players who generate large incomes and demand a significant say over the way that their sport is run. Relying on such a dividing line, Szymanski's analysis identifies two current financial crises in European sports, one concerning professional sports such as football, the other hitting local grassroots sports clubs. In the first case, clubs overspend on player talents in the pursuit of success, putting themselves in financial jeopardy: around 50 English football clubs have entered into administration. Even those European leagues where football clubs have tighter financial regulation have not escaped financial crisis. On the other hand, grassroots sports clubs are in crisis because it has become harder to obtain public subsidies, due to fiscal deficit, and membership and volunteerism are under pressure.

Then the governance issue comes to the fore. Professional clubs want a bigger say in the running of national federations, to reflect the significance of their financial contributions, and their wealthy and powerful owners have little reverence for national traditions in sport, while in some countries the government steps in to fill the income gap between professional and grassroots sports. Thus Szymanski contends that the state is 'the elephant in the room' in a pyramidal European model of sport. Sports federations tend to see government as a source of finance, but resist the attempts of government to impose its priorities, whereas governments tend to consider federations as fully representative of all sport, thus neglecting the role of both business and autonomous self-organised (by the participants) sports. In conclusion, the chapter presents a matrix model of European sport which is more likely to capture the roots of its current crisis.

While in European sport systems, taxation and revenue redistribution in the form of subsidies from the richest professional sports are basically public, as Szymanski argues, in North American sports, a 'private' taxation and revenue distribution is confined to intra-league mechanisms. One case in point is the so-called luxury tax applied to the highest spending teams in a league when their payroll is in excess of a defined threshold. Joel Maxcy reminds us that the 1997 collective bargaining agreement between the Major League Baseball (MLB) owners and the players' union introduced a luxury tax on club payrolls, renamed the competitive balance tax since 2006, for the purpose of enhancing competitive balance (Chapter 5). From his theoretical model, Maxcy concludes that a luxury tax reduces the incentive to hire talent beyond the tax threshold. Then an empirical model of player transfers in the context of a luxury tax is developed and tested with MLB data, since changes in the distribution of talent can be evidenced in detail by player mobility across clubs. Contrary to popular wisdom, the results provide general support for the effectiveness of the luxury tax in restraining spending by high revenue teams.

Another follow-up to Szymanski's chapter is that a new source of money is flowing into sport at a skyrocketing pace: betting and gambling on sporting outcomes. However, it is not without its problem since one single sport betting company is (or was, as in Germany) a public monopoly in various European countries in order to prevent people from developing a pathological gambling addiction. On the other hand, levying a percentage on the public betting company's sales is an easy channel for transferring some monies to the government sports budget or, as in France, to some para-fiscal fund that supplements a tiny sports budget. Such a channel is used to finance grassroots sports, but now the sport betting industry has to be open to competition in compliance with EU deregulation. A threat is felt by all in the sport movement, basically at grassroots level, while sport betting in Europe will become a fully-fledged market activity in the near future.

Frank Daumann and Markus Breuer (Chapter 6) use the sport betting markets – where information is processed by bookmakers to enhance forecasts about sporting outcomes – for testing market efficiency. Information is differentiated into three subsets: information known before the season (long-term performance of a team), information influencing the winning probability and becoming obvious during a match (which cannot be used to forecast winning probabilities), and relevant information which becomes public during the current season (dependent on time). Postulating an efficient utilisation of available information, Daumann and Breuer ask whether the quality of the forecasts would improve during a sport season. Calculating win probabilities, they find some surprising results. Bookmaker forecasts are not better than those obtained only by chance. The assumption of an increasing quality of forecasting over the sport season is not verified. However such conclusions cannot be generalised due to the limited size of the matchday sample. One of the rather provocative implications derived by the authors is that a football match outcome may well depend on chance to a large extent. This challenges the current view that a team performance is closely linked to its financial possibilities, if not in the long run, at least on a matchday or even during a season.

Football pools in the gambling market in Spain are also used as a new source of revenue for the government to further promote sporting activities. Revenues from football pools channel significant investment into football-related social causes. Since revenues are a fixed proportion of sales, Jaume García, Levi Pérez and Plácido Rodríguez (Chapter 7) investigate whether football pools managers adopt a revenue-maximising objective in looking at the determinants of participation such as price, the size of the prize pool and the difficulty of the game. The composition of betting coupons, in terms of teams included, is also taken into account. Two modes of betting can be offered to the bettors: the effective price model and the jackpot model. This may influence the demand for football pools in Spain, the determinants of which are analysed in this chapter. The jackpot from one fixture to the next one induces variation in the top prize as well as in the expected return. The composition of betting coupons is expected to affect participation strongly, the expectation being that the teams included in each bet represent a decisive determinant of participation and act as a key variable of football pools management.

The major results drawn from an OLS estimation of both effective price and jackpot models with instrumental variables show that individuals betting on the exact score are more loyal and skilled bettors than those just guessing which team wins. For both games (score or win betting), the jackpot model fits the data better than the effective price model. Considering long-run price elasticity of sales, *El Quinigol* (score betting) implies revenue maximisation while *La Quiniela* (win betting) could increase its revenues by changing the game design. In the short term, bets in *El Quinigol* are quite sensitive to changes in the effective price instead of increases in the jackpot. Not including First Division teams in the betting coupon has a relatively important (negative) impact on sales for win betting but a quite small effect on sales for score betting.

In the final chapter, Wladimir Andreff and Gaël Raballand start from the evidence of an increasing percentage of games resulting in a 0–0 draw or a 1–0 win in the five major European football leagues. They first check that any explanation of such a trend cannot be found in the literature about competitive balance and game attendance (and find very few references), while both may be affected by the trend towards low scoring on the pitch. Then they gather theoretical evidence, relying on Groot's work (2008), and empirical evidence showing that lower goal scoring has slowed down competitive balance deterioration in European football. The low goal scoring trend in European football appears to be an historical one since it is triggered by increasingly defensive tactics on the pitch over many decades. Such a trend has not been countervailed by a change in FIFA rules (three points for a win), expected to produce more goals per game, fewer draws, and on top of this, more exciting games that attract more interest. Some theoretical reasons why such a measure has been counterproductive – or at least ineffective – are surveyed, together with blurred evidence derived from econometric testing so far.

Then a regression analysis is run on data on the five major European football leagues in order to check whether competitive balance is determined by goal scoring variables whilst controlling for defensive–attacking tactics, and specific league and year variables.

This inception study on a new topic exhibits the following preliminary results: team standing is improved by its defensive tactics, is negatively affected by 0–0 draws and is positively affected by 1–0 wins, but the effect of low goal scoring and defensive tactics on competitive balance is more significant in some leagues (like the French *Ligue 1*) than others, such as the German *Bundesliga*. Avenues for further research are suggested to test whether there is a trade-off for a league between attracting attendance with an improved competitive balance and scoring attractiveness, since competitive balance improves with growing 0–0 and 1–0 scores.

NOTES

1. The *Journal of Sports Economics* (since 2000) and the *International Journal of Sport Finance* (since 2006) provide two new publication options. Before 2000, economists had little opportunity to publish in the area of sports economics in either general economic journals or sport management journals; just one, the *European Journal of Sport Management*, was open to economic articles. It was established in 1992, and in 2001 became the *European Sport Management Quarterly*.
2. A summarised version of this study with an update regarding the impact of the current global financial crisis on sports finance was presented at a WEAI conference (Andreff, 2009).
3. See the special issue of the *Journal of Sports Economics* (vol. 7, no. 1, 2006) and a follow-up in vol. 8, no. 6, 2007, including Andreff (2007a).

REFERENCES

Amnyos (2008), *Etude du financement public et privé du sport*, State Secretary for Sports, Paris, October.
Andreff, W. (1981), 'Les inégalités entre les disciplines sportives: une approche économique', in C. Pociello (ed.), *Sports et société*, Paris: Vigot, 139–51.
Andreff, W. (2007a), 'French Football: A Financial Crisis Rooted in Weak Governance', *Journal of Sports Economics*, **8**, 652–61.
Andreff, W. (2007b), 'Governance Issues in French Professional Football', in P. Rodriguez, S. Késenne and J. Garcia (eds), *Governance and Competition in Professional Sports Leagues*, Oviedo: Ediciones de la Universidad de Oviedo, 55–86.
Andreff, W. (2009), 'Public and Private Financing of Sport in Europe: The Impact of Global Crisis', paper presented at the *84th Annual Conference of Western Economic Association International*, Vancouver, 29 June–3 July.

Andreff, W. (forthcoming) (ed.), *Recent Development in Sports Economics*, Cheltenham: Edward Elgar.

Andreff, W., Bourg, J.-F., Halba, B. and Nys, J.-F. (1994), 'The Economic Importance of Sport in Europe: Financing and Economic Impact', Background document to the *14th Informal Meeting of European Sports Ministers*, Council of Europe, Strasbourg, April.

Andreff, W. and Staudohar, P. (2000), 'The Evolving European Model of Professional Sports Finance', *Journal of Sports Economics*, **1** (3), 257–76.

Andreff, W. and Szymanski, S. (2006) (eds), *Handbook on the Economics of Sport*, Cheltenham: Edward Elgar.

Downward, P., Dawson, A. and Dejonghe, T. (2009), *Sports Economics: Theory, Evidence and Policy*, London: Butterworth-Heinemann.

Fort, R. (2003), *Sports Economics*, Upper Saddle River, NJ: Prentice Hall.

Groot, L. (2008), *Economics, Uncertainty and European Football: Trends in Competitive Balance*, Cheltenham: Edward Elgar.

Késenne, S. (2007), *The Economic Theory of Professional Team Sports: An Analytical Treatment*, Cheltenham: Edward Elgar.

Leeds, M. and von Allmen, P. (2002), *The Economics of Sports*, Boston, MA: Addison Wesley.

Rottenberg, S. (1956), 'The Baseball Players' Labor Market', *Journal of Political Economy*, **64**, 242–58.

Sandy, R., Sloane, P.J. and Rosentraub, M.S. (2004), *The Economics of Sport: An International Perspective*, Basingstoke: Palgrave Macmillan.

Zimbalist, A. (2001) (ed.), *The Economics of Sport*, Cheltenham: Edward Elgar.

PART I

Economic analysis of sport participation determinants and social impact

2. Participation, spectatorship and media coverage in sport: some initial insights

Peter Dawson and Paul Downward

INTRODUCTION

Current sports policy in the UK emphasizes a symbiotic link between the hosting of major sports events and participation in sport (DCMS/Strategy Unit, 2002). Implicitly, it is maintained that viewing sports events live or via the media is the key to revealing latent demand for active participation. Such hypothesized links have not, however, been analysed in the literature, with the implication that such claims lack an evidence base. Using an econometric model, this chapter explores official data in the UK and finds robust evidence that sports participation and sports spectatorship are symbiotically linked.

The chapter proceeds as follows. Section 2 briefly reviews the policy context of the current research. Section 3 reviews the literature on sports participation, and on spectating at events, live and through the media. Section 4 discusses the data and variables used in the current study. Section 5 provides details on the econometric methods employed and the results and discussion are presented in Section 6. Conclusions then follow.

POLICY CONTEXT

As detailed in Gratton and Taylor (2000) and Downward *et al.* (2009) the sports economy comprises a series of interconnected sectors that embrace professional team sports, sports events and mass participation. In the former two contexts, sport is consumed by spectators either in a live setting, or live or recorded via the media. As is well documented in the professional team sport literature (Borland and MacDonald, 2003; Downward *et al.*, 2009) competitors produce a contest which can be regarded as a joint product. This, of course, also applies to events. The essential difference between sports events and professional team sports, therefore, is that the latter are organized by teams in cartel leagues with a regular series of fixtures, whereas the former are more irregular sporting encounters, of a more limited duration than a season, and can embrace more than one sport. Sports leagues and sports events can operate at both the elite and non-elite levels.[1]

As Gratton and Taylor (2000) note, sports events can be classified according to different criteria, such as their regularity and their significance in both sporting terms and the level of economic activity that they generate. For example, most sports have some form of annual national championships, and most, but particularly younger-age championships, have relatively little economic activity associated with them, as the spectators are primarily connected to the sports participants. The participants moreover are more likely to be amateur and not necessarily elite. In contrast, events such as Formula 1 Grand Prix, Wimbledon tennis, and Six Nations Rugby internationals generate much more economic activity as they are major spectator events involving elite professional athletes. Likewise, whereas some multisport events have sporting but little economic significance, such as meets of the International Amateur Athletics Federation (IAAF), events such as the Olympic and Commonwealth Games have much greater economic activity associated with them.[2] Clearly this also applies to events such as the World Cup in various sports.

The remaining sector of the sports economy comprises mass participation activity. Broadly speaking, from an economic perspective, this involves the consumption of sport as participation by consumer-producers who allocate time and market goods to the pursuit of the relevant activity (Downward *et al.*, 2009). Nonetheless, external (to the producer) supply opportunities vary for the consumer. They can involve completely informal activity by individuals and self-chosen groups being undertaken in public spaces such as parks or the neighbourhood or in their own private spaces, such as gardens. Activity can also take place in leisure facilities provided by the public or private sector in which the participant acts as a customer.[3] Finally, and common to most countries, participation can occur through formalized sports-club systems that are the origins of many professional sports organizations, and which restrict access according to some form of membership criteria (Downward *et al.*, 2009). These sectors have evolved and remain connected in a complex way which is of significance for both governing bodies and current UK sports policy.

The latter underwent a significant overhaul following the publication of *Game Plan: A Strategy for Delivering Government's Sport and Physical Activity Objectives* in 2002 (DCMS/Strategy Unit, 2002). This document identified the two main and allegedly symbiotic objectives for government sport policy discussed in the introduction (p12), which have recently been reaffirmed in *Playing to Win: A New Era for Sport* (DCMS, 2008). They include increasing participation in sport and physical activity, primarily because of the significant health benefits and to reduce the growing costs of inactivity, and also to achieve a sustainable improvement in success in international competition, particularly in the sports which matter most to the public, primarily because of the 'feel-good factor' associated with winning. Impacts from the latter will then have an impact on the former. Naturally, such policy sentiments underpinned the London 2012 bid and the desire for the UK to host other events.

Despite these policy priorities, however, there has been little critical reflection on the likely feedback between sports participation and event spectatorship (of any type and either live or on TV). However, it is highly likely that many of the consumer-producers of mass participation sport are also consumers of sport at live events, and/or through the media. Significantly, there is no substantive research that addresses these issues. The following literature review exemplifies this situation.

LITERATURE REVIEW

The literature on sports demands has three discrete emphases: the attendance demand for professional sports, participation demand, and spectatorship at major sports events. The attendance demand for professional sports leagues is extremely well researched and summarized in Borland and MacDonald (2003) and Downward *et al.* (2009). The main findings of the literature include that demand is generally found to be price, and to a lesser extent income inelastic. The market size of teams is ubiquitously significant as are measures of team quality, the success of teams, favourable weather, local rivalries, matches that have sporting significance (such as local derbies), and the rescheduling of games away from traditional times and days, for example as broadcasting income has reshaped traditional competitions. There is some growing evidence that uncertainty of outcome stimulates demand, but the results are mixed, as are those for the effects of habit persistence on attendance.

Of particular significance for this chapter is the impact of broadcast media on attendance demand, and also the broadcasting demand for sport. In the former case the historical literature indicates some mixed results; however, more recent literature has shown that once the rescheduling of matches that often occurs with TV broadcasts is controlled for, there is some evidence of a substitution effect on attendances. However, it is also argued that whilst televised games reduce attendances, overall the televised games are correspondent with increased revenues for the clubs in the Premier League and First Division (see Baimbridge *et al.*, 1996; Forrest *et al.*, 2004). In the second instance, as far as the media demand for sport is concerned, research in economics is scant, though two innovative studies, Forrest et al. (2005) and Alavy et al. (2006), examine the choice of broadcasters to televise a game and broadcast viewing figures on a minute-by-minute basis respectively. In the former case it is shown that in the second half of the season, in which broadcasters have more discretion over the games that are televised, uncertainty of outcome increases the likelihood of a game being shown live. In the latter case it is shown that viewers prefer eventful contests with a result rather than uncertain outcomes and 'tame draws'. In general, however, this literature does not examine this demand in connection with spectatorship at live matches, or participation in sport. One important exception is Buraimo (2008), who examines the joint demand of English Football League match day and broadcasting attendances. It is concluded that whilst broadcasting matches reduces match day attendance, there is positive feedback, such that larger attendances have positive impacts on broadcasting audiences.[4]

There is now a growing international literature examining sports participation (Lera-López and Rapún-Gárate, 2005; Stratton *et al.*, 2005; Humphreys and Ruseski, 2006; Taks and Scheerder, 2006;

Downward and Riordan, 2007; Wicker, Breuer and Pawlowski, 2009; Downward and Rasciute, 2010). The general findings of the literature are that males tend to participate more in sport than females, except in particular aesthetic activities as well as games that developed as female sports. Lower age, higher incomes and higher socio-economic status also raise the participation rate in sports. The same is true of health, being self-reported as better for respondents, and levels of education being higher. A variety of household characteristics also appear to reduce participation in sport. These include being married or a couple and, particularly, the presence of children in the household. However, participation in other sports activities or having active family members does promote sports participation Finally, there is evidence that increased work hours can reduce participation rates, as can being of a non-white ethnicity. Whilst it is recognized that there are possible substitute relationships in sports participation, the relatively sparse literature examines other leisure activities and not live and media sports spectatorship (Kesenne, 1981, 1983; Kesenne and Butzen, 1987; Downward and Rasciute, 2010).

Finally, the literature on attendance demand at live sports events, as distinct from sports leagues, is relatively undeveloped. Most of the literature on sports events is connected with economic impacts and, consequently, refining which elements of spectator demand (and expenditures) should legitimately be measured (Crompton, 1995, 2006; Preuss, 2004). The literature which examines behaviour has tended to develop out of sports tourism research and, particularly, is concerned with exploring the motivations to attend events (for example see: Giulianotti, 1995; Hunt, Bristol and Bashaw, 1999; Mahony, Madrigal and Howard, 2000; Trail, Anderson and Fink, 2000; Funk and James, 2001; Clowes and Tapp, 2003; Crawford, 2003; Stewart, Smith and Nicholson, 2003; Trail, Fink and Anderson, 2003; Campbell, Aiken and Kent, 2004) as well as taxonomies of sports tourist (Glyptis, 1982; Weed and Bull, 2004) and distinguishing between active participants and passive spectators (Weed and Bull, 2004). However, none of this work has explored the relationships *between* sports demands either. Consequently, it is to address these gaps in the literature that this chapter develops a model of sports participation that explicitly accounts for both spectating at live sports events as well as the TV coverage of sports (and TV watching generally).

DATA AND VARIABLES

To model the relationships between sports participation, spectating at sports live at events and watching sports on TV, data from the first tranche of the DCMS Taking Part Survey from 2005, and now lodged in the Data Archive for public access, is analysed. This was a three-year survey, completed in 2008, and collected data on participation in culture, leisure and sport in England for adults aged 16 years and over.[5] The first tranche of data comprised 28 117 respondents. Data was collected by individual interview concerning participation or not over the last four weeks and also the 12 months prior to the interview. For the former data, the frequency of participation is also available in the form of days, hours and minutes. Each of these frequency measures is explored in the empirical analysis that follows.

The dataset also includes information on spectator demand and TV viewing habits. The key covariates are a binary variable measuring if the respondent has attended a live sports event in the last four weeks as a spectator or not, and two binary variables measuring if the respondent watches live sport on TV or not, or other sport on TV or not. As well as sport TV viewing, higher levels of general TV viewing are also included in the analysis, as TV viewing comprises the largest passive leisure activity and is, of course, a substitute activity for sports viewing. Higher levels of TV viewing are measured by a series of binary variables.

Table 2.1 reports mean participation rates by minutes, hours and days for all sports for general TV viewing, sports viewing on TV and also attendance at a sports event. The data show that those who watch five or more hours of TV a day participate nearly 50 per cent less than those respondents who watch TV for less than 1 hour per day. However, the effect of watching sport on TV is positively associated with participation. These unconditional figures suggest the impact is greater for non-live, as opposed to live events. Spectating at live sporting events also appears to have complementary effects on participation. The sample size for the table is set at 12 370 cases, which is less than the total size of the dataset. This is because it reflects the maximum sample size available without missing cases across the broad set of covariates used in the analysis.

As well as the covariates just discussed, in the empirical analysis that follows we include a variety of covariates which capture

Table 2.1   *Mean participation rates by TV viewing habits and spectator demand*

Characteristic	Minutes	Hours	Days
TV Viewing Habits	Sports Participation		
TV less than 1 hour	769.35	12.82	10.46
TV 1 hour	659.84	11.00	8.71
TV 2 hours	589.73	9.83	7.84
TV 3 hours	577.37	9.62	7.20
TV 4 hours	516.78	8.61	6.20
TV 5 or more hours	401.90	6.70	4.90
TV live sport	727.34	12.12	8.73
TV any sport	798.71	13.31	9.25
Spectator Demand			
Attended a live sporting event	873.17	14.55	10.82

Note: N = 12 370

socio-economic and demographic characteristics associated with participation in sport. These include the usual variables associated with age, income, gender, marital status and household dynamics (number and composition of people in the household). Table 2.2 provides a full list of the covariates used in this chapter together with their sample means and standard deviations.

ECONOMETRIC METHODOLOGY

To model the participation decision, previous studies have concentrated on some form of binary choice models. Typically, a logit-type estimation approach is carried out in order to ascertain the probability (or odds) of participating in sport or physical activity. Often this modelling has formed part of an analysis of frequency of participation using some form of sample selection model, typically a Heckman model (Heckman, 1979). In fact, a number of alternative sample selection models could be employed in this respect. Standard Tobit models (Tobit Type I models) are the most traditional possibility but restrict the signs and covariates on the selection and frequency variables, and also rely heavily on the normality of residuals. In this regard the literature's use of a Heckman model (Tobit Type

Table 2.2   Variable labels, definitions and summary statistics

Variable Label	Definition	Mean	Standard Deviation
Socio-Economic and Demographic Characteristics			
SINGLE	1 if respondent has never been married, 0 otherwise	0.324	0.468
MARRIED	1 if respondent is married, 0 otherwise	0.489	0.500
ASIAN	1 if respondent is Asian, 0 otherwise	0.069	0.254
BLACK	1 if respondent is black, 0 otherwise	0.045	0.208
OTHERETH	1 if respondent is from another ethnic minority, 0 otherwise	0.026	0.156
NORTHE	1 if respondent lives in North East	0.092	0.289
NORTHW	1 if respondent lives in North West	0.102	0.303
YORKS	1 if respondent lives in Yorkshire	0.105	0.306
EMID	1 if respondent lives in East Midlands	0.088	0.283
WMID	1 if respondent lives in West Midlands	0.115	0.319
EAST	1 if respondent lives in East England	0.107	0.309
SOUTHE	1 if respondent lives in South East	0.153	0.360
SOUTHW	1 if respondent lives in South West	0.114	0.318
WORKING	1 if respondent is in employment, 0 otherwise	0.668	0.471
STUDENT	1 if respondent is a full-time student, 0 otherwise	0.032	0.175
KEEPHOUSE	1if respondent keeps house, 0 otherwise	0.068	0.251
RETIRED	1 if respondent is retired, 0 otherwise	0.150	0.357
ILLNOTWORK	1 if respondent is ill and cannot work, 0 otherwise	0.030	0.171

Variable Label	Definition	Mean	Standard Deviation
HE	Higher education or equivalent = 1, 0 otherwise	0.420	0.494
ALEVEL	1 if respondent has A Levels, 0 otherwise	0.198	0.399
MALE	1 if male, 0 female	0.464	0.499
AGE	Age of respondent	43.638	16.230
DRINKDAILY	1 if respondent drinks alcohol every day, 0 otherwise	0.103	0.304
SMKDAILY	1 if respondent smokes every day, 0 otherwise	0.206	0.404
GENHEALTH	Self-reported general health: 1 very poor, 5 very good	4.105	0.849
NADULT	Number of adults in household	1.981	0.845
NCHILD	Number of children in household	0.665	1.000
LOGINCOME	Log of personal earnings in the last year before tax and other deductions (mid-point)	9.039	2.273

Leisure and TV Viewing Habit Variables

Variable Label	Definition	Mean	Standard Deviation
SPCLOSE	1 if sports facility within 20 minutes	0.943	0.233
VOLUNTARY	1 if respondent has undertaken voluntary work within the last 12 months	0.278	0.448
LIVESPORT	1 if respondent has attended a live sporting event in the last 4 weeks (as a spectator)	0.156	0.363
TV1HR	1 if respondent watches TV about 1 hour a day	0.135	0.342
TV2HR	1 if respondent watches TV about 2 hours a day	0.298	0.457
TV3HR	1 if respondent watches TV about 3 hours a day	0.239	0.427
TV4HR	1 if respondent watches TV about 4 hours a day	0.138	0.345
TV5PLUS	1 if respondent watches TV about 5 or more hours a day	0.106	0.308

Table 2.2   (continued)

Variable Label	Definition	Mean	Standard Deviation
TVLIVESPORT	1 if respondent watches live sport on TV	0.516	0.500
TVOTHERSPORT	1 if respondent watches other (non-live) sport on TV	0.272	0.445

Note: N = 12 370

II) is more flexible in that the signs and covariates in the two-part modelling are not restricted to be the same. However, as pointed out by Downward and Riordan (2007), one major disadvantage of the Heckman approach is that in cross-section data and reduced form estimation, finding variables that are excluded from the frequency equation but not the probability of participation equation as an identifying restriction is difficult and, in fact, arbitrary in many official data sets. To some extent the same problems would be present with Hurdle models (Mullahy, 1986).

In contrast, the econometric strategy employed in this chapter is to use count data models. In part this reflects the desire to estimate a single reduced form equation without the employment of arbitrary identification and in part because we have information on the frequency of participation in days, hours or minutes. Frequency of sport participation by minute, hour and number of days are displayed in Figures 2.1, 2.2 and 2.3, respectively.[6]

The figures clearly display a left-skewed distribution with a high fraction of zero outcomes. In these cases, traditional modelling approaches such as OLS are likely to lead to biased estimates. Further converting the data into a discrete form is not desirable since this will invariably lead to a loss of information. Despite the broadly continuous nature of some of the alternative dependent variables (minutes and hours) the most appropriate methods of dealing with such a distribution can be argued to be count models. Wooldridge (2002), for example, has argued that count models can be applied to non-negative continuous variables and negates the use of log transformation (for example, $\log(1 + y)$) which leads to problems in calculating the expected value of y.

The simplest count model is based on the Poisson distribution:

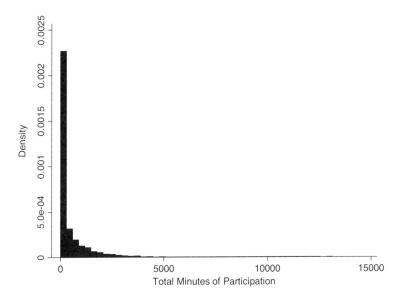

Figure 2.1   Participation in sport (total minutes)

$$p(y_i) = \frac{\lambda_i^{y_i} e^{-\lambda_i}}{y_i!} \tag{2.1}$$

where y_i refers to the frequency of participation (days, hours or minutes) in sport or physical activity. λ is linked to an exponential function of the set of covariates:

$$\lambda_i = e^{\beta' x_i + \delta' z} \tag{2.2}$$

where k is the number of covariates and x_i is the $1 \times k$ row vector of covariates with corresponding parameter vector b.

One important limitation of the standard Poisson model is the assumption of equidispersion, which states that the conditional mean of the dependent variable is equal to its conditional variance. In many applications, it is often the case that the conditional variance exceeds the conditional mean, which means the dependent variable is over-dispersed. In order to correct for over-dispersion, a popular alternative is the negative binomial regression (NBR) model. It is obtained as a mixture density (Cameron and Trivedi, 2005; Greene, 2008):

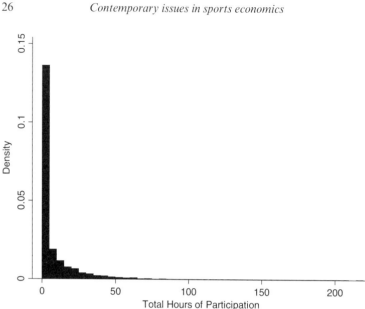

Figure 2.2   Participation in sport (total hours)

$$p(y_i) = \frac{\Gamma(\theta_i + y_i)}{\Gamma(y_i + 1)\Gamma(\theta_i)} \left(\frac{\lambda_i}{\lambda_i + \theta_i}\right)^{y_i} \left(\frac{\theta_i}{\lambda_i + \theta_i}\right)^{\theta_i} \quad (2.3)$$

where Γ is the gamma function and λ_i is linked to the same set of covariates as identified in (2.2). θ_i is a parameter that determines the degree of dispersion. For the purpose of identification it is assumed to be the same for all individuals. A common formulation is to assume: $\theta_i = \alpha^{-1}$. In this case the conditional mean is $E(y_i) = \lambda_i$ and the conditional variance is $Var(y_i) = \lambda_i(1 + 1/\alpha^{-1}\lambda_i)$. A statistical test on a determines the appropriateness of the NBR model over the Poisson model, and hence whether there is over- (or under-) dispersion in the dependent variable.

A specific problem in both Poisson and NBR models occurs when the dependent variable has an overabundance of zeros; this generally leads to both the Poisson and NBR under-predicting the number of zeros. One solution to this problem is to employ a zero-inflated model; this considers the existence of two latent groups within the population: one group has zero counts and the other group has

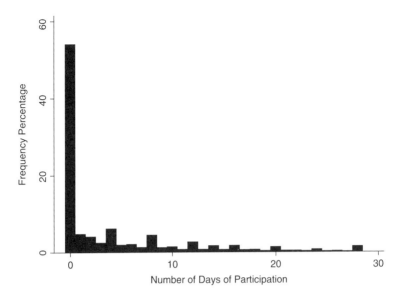

Figure 2.3   Participation in sport (total days)

strictly positive counts. Consequently estimation proceeds in two parts. In the case of the Poisson, we have:

$$p(y_i = 0) = \eta_i + (1 - \eta_i)e^{-\lambda_i} \tag{2.4a}$$

$$p(y_i > 0) = (1 - \eta_i)\frac{\lambda_i^{y_i}e^{-\lambda_i}}{y_i} \tag{2.4b}$$

and for the NBR:

$$p(y_i = 0) = \eta_i + (1 - \eta_i)\left(\frac{\theta_i}{\lambda_i + \theta_i}\right)^{\theta_i} \tag{2.5a}$$

$$p(y_i > 0) = (1 - \eta_i)\frac{\Gamma(\theta_i + y_i)}{\Gamma(y_i + 1)\Gamma(\theta_i)}\left(\frac{\lambda_i}{\lambda_i + \theta_i}\right)^{y_i}\left(\frac{\theta_i}{\lambda_i + \theta_i}\right)^{\theta_i} \tag{2.5b}$$

where, as before, λ_i is linked to an exponential function of the set of covariates.

This discussion leads to a further reason for employing count data models in the current context. The idea that the zeros are generated from more than one source is particularly appealing in the case of participation in sport and the use of official data sets. It is possible that a zero could have arisen either because the respondent did not participate in the four weeks prior to interview (but had done so in a previous period) or the respondent had never participated. In order to establish statistically the appropriateness of a zero-inflated model, the non-nested test suggested by Vuong (1989) can be used.

RESULTS[7]

In this study, attention is confined to the overall levels of participation aggregated across all sports. Using standard OLS, Model 1 in Table 2.3 presents the results of the frequency of participation in minutes with robust standard errors. Many of the parameters on the variables are in line with previous studies. In particular, participation declines with age, number of children, those who are working and those who are married. Males, on average, participate 341 minutes more than females. The results relating to TV viewing habits also conform to prior expectations: just one hour of TV viewing per day decreases participation on average by 108 minutes (over a four-week period). This figure rises to 274 minutes for those who watch for five or more hours per day.

The variables broadly described as relating to watching sport all have positive and statistically significant effects on participation. Attendance at one or more live sporting event during the previous four weeks has the largest impact, increasing participation, on average, by 171 minutes. The positive effect associated with watching sport (live or otherwise) on TV suggests that whilst TV in general is a substitute for participation, sport on TV acts as a complement.

The inclusion of month dummies and weighting the observations (Model 2) generally have the effect of attenuating the results both in terms of the size of coefficients and the level of significance, but nonetheless they are comparable to Model 1. In Models 3 and 4, minutes of participation are replaced with hours and days, respectively. Whilst Model 3 is essentially a scaled version of Model 2, some differences are observed when the dependent variable is days of participation. For example, in Model 4, and unlike previous models, both education (positive) and smoking (negative) are now statistically significant.

The various count models for hours and days of participation are presented in Tables 2.4 and 2.5 respectively.[8] The estimates for the basic Poisson models appear to generate suspiciously small stand-ard errors and therefore very large z-scores. There are only three variables that are not statistically significant at the 5 per cent level or better (in the case of the earlier OLS model, there were around 17 variables deemed to be insignificant).

Due to the scepticism of the results reported in the Poisson model, and in order to better control for unobserved heterogeneity, the NBR model was estimated. The results are consistent with the OLS results presented in Table 2.3. Age, number of children and those working remained negatively associated with participation whereas males, number of people in the household and health status are posi-tively associated with participation. TV viewing habits and watch-ing sport also remain important: those who go to watch live sport increase their hours of participation by about 20 per cent (or about 15 per cent more days) than those who do not. Similar magnitudes are found for those respondents who watch live sport on TV.

Because of the presence of an overabundance of zeros, both Poisson and NBR models are likely to under-predict the number of zeros. To overcome this, zero-inflated Poisson (ZIP) and zero-inflated negative binomial (ZINB) models were estimated. The zero-inflated models generate two sets of coefficients: one set for the binary model, which establishes respondents having zero levels of participation, and one set for the Poisson or negative binomial parts, which predicts the counts for the respondents with positive levels of participation. In the cases presented here, we use the logit specifi-cation for the binary model.

Because the binary model is predicated on establishing the deter-minants of a zero level of participation, the signs of the coefficients tend to be opposite those in the Poisson and negative binomial parts. Once again, however, our results suggest that there are one or two anomalies. For example, the probability of non-participation is higher for those respondents who smoke daily, but it is also posi-tively associated with the frequency of participation (in the case of hours of participation but not days of participation). According to the results of the ZINB model, and similar to our finding in the NBR model, attendance at live sporting events has a similar effect to watching live sport on TV. Attendance at live sporting events does however exert a greater influence on the probability of participation.

In order to determine which of the various count models is the most appropriate, Figures 2.4 and 2.5 plot the residuals from the

Table 2.3 Frequency of participation: OLS estimates

Variable	Model 1 (Minutes)	Model 2 (Minutes)	Model 3 (Hours)	Model 4 (Days)
SINGLE	−45.38 (29.74)	−6.95 (40.01)	−0.12 (0.67)	−0.20 (0.25)
MARRIED	−171.62*** (28.53)	−162.17*** (33.49)	−2.70*** (0.56)	−0.77*** (0.21)
ASIAN	−125.40*** (37.72)	−130.55*** (49.46)	−2.18*** (0.82)	−0.24 (0.31)
BLACK	−83.40 (53.50)	−119.90* (69.60)	−2.00* (−1.16)	−0.74* (0.44)
OTHERETH	−24.20 (72.85)	−83.01 (68.34)	−1.38 (1.14)	−1.20** (0.44)
NORTHE	−9.14 (43.89)	30.99 (52.18)	0.52 (0.87)	−0.05 (0.33)
NORTHW	23.93 (45.60)	48.46 (40.34)	0.81 (0.67)	−0.25 (0.26)
YORKS	−56.16 (42.08)	−32.64 (42.39)	−0.54 (0.71)	−0.50 (0.27)
EMID	18.89 (47.31)	45.20 (44.92)	0.75 (0.75)	−0.34 (0.29)
WMID	−113.00*** (37.69)	−116.74*** (41.19)	−1.95*** (0.69)	−0.54 (0.26)
EAST	−22.85 (41.31)	−2.69 (40.94)	−0.04 (0.68)	−0.43* (0.26)
SOUTHE	−60.14 (37.51)	−40.55 (35.90)	−0.68 (0.60)	−0.52** (0.23)
SOUTHW	−38.66 (41.58)	−12.03 (41.57)	−0.20 (0.69)	−0.37 (0.26)
WORKING	−124.31** (51.34)	−77.25* (46.40)	−1.29* (0.77)	−0.01 (0.30)
STUDENT	−55.80 (95.13)	−132.76* (68.22)	−2.13* (1.14)	−0.74 (0.44)
KEEPHOUSE	−141.75* (57.39)	−74.94 (62.23)	−1.25 (1.04)	−0.81** (0.39)
RETIRED	115.37* (58.81)	195.98*** (59.72)	3.27*** (1.00)	1.04** (0.38)
ILLNOTWORK	−102.32 (63.80)	−74.41 (79.40)	−1.24 (1.32)	−0.46 (0.50)
HE	36.36* (21.99)	−10.43 (24.00)	−0.17 (0.40)	0.64*** (0.151)
ALEVEL	32.67 (27.23)	−12.46 (27.56)	−0.21 (0.46)	0.30* (0.17)
MALE	341.38*** (21.63)	376.89*** (22.35)	6.28*** (0.37)	1.03*** (0.14)
AGE	−14.83*** (1.033)	−15.40*** (1.10)	−0.26*** (0.02)	−0.10*** (0.01)

DRINKDAILY	13.76 (31.08)	19.10 (33.94)	0.32 (0.57)	0.29 (0.21)
SMKDAILY	−13.13 (26.51)	26.36 (25.84)	0.44 (0.43)	−0.75*** (0.16)
GENHEALTH	141.20*** (11.56)	157.92*** (13.24)	2.63*** (0.22)	0.85*** (0.08)
NADULT	96.21*** (16.57)	102.99*** (12.00)	1.72*** (0.20)	0.24*** (0.08)
NCHILD	−56.11*** (11.84)	−55.45*** (11.72)	−0.92*** (0.20)	−0.21*** (0.07)
LOGINCOME	−7.28 (5.01)	−9.30* (5.19)	−0.16* (0.09)	−0.05 (0.03)
SPCLOSE	132.71*** (34.95)	167.83*** (27.35)	2.80*** (0.75)	1.20*** (0.28)
VOLUNTARY	156.81*** (23.19)	194.19*** (22.79)	3.24*** (0.38)	1.04*** (0.15)
LIVESPORT	171.50*** (30.56)	176.41*** (27.35)	2.94*** (0.46)	0.86*** (0.18)
TV1HR	−108.47** (48.57)	−71.34* (42.83)	−1.19* (0.71)	−0.24 (0.28)
TV2HR	−157.77*** (44.11)	−151.64*** (38.46)	−2.53*** (0.64)	−0.82*** (0.25)
TV3HR	−174.25*** (45.37)	−152.14*** (40.01)	−2.54*** (0.67)	−1.02*** (0.26)
TV4HR	−209.39*** (48.86)	−208.85*** (44.46)	−3.48*** (0.74)	−1.54*** (0.29)
TV5PLUS	−274.11*** (50.98)	−239.33*** (48.83)	−3.99*** (0.81)	−1.89*** (0.31)
TVLIVESPORT	138.86*** (21.50)	148.48*** (23.80)	2.47*** (0.40)	0.72*** (0.15)
TVOTHERSPORT	116.34*** (26.80)	118.80*** (25.79)	1.98*** (0.43)	0.89*** (0.16)
CONSTANT	468.80*** (112.23)	−127.62 (435.28)	−2.13 (7.25)	5.03* (2.7)
MONTH DUMMIES	NO	YES	YES	YES
WEIGHTS	NO	YES	YES	YES
N	12370	12370	12370	11930

Notes: standard errors in parentheses. */**/***, denote significant at 10%, 5% and 1% level respectively.

Table 2.4   Hours of participation: alternative count models

Variable	Poisson	Negative Binomial	Zero-inflated Poisson		Zero-inflated Negative Binomial	
			Logit	Poisson	Logit	Neg Bin
SINGLE	-0.04*** (0.01)	-0.07 (0.07)	0.18*** (0.07)	-0.01 (0.01)	0.25*** (0.09)	-0.0004 (0.05)
MARRIED	-0.18*** (0.01)	-0.09* (0.06)	0.10 (0.06)	-0.16*** (0.01)	0.06 (0.08)	-0.15*** (0.05)
ASIAN	-0.15*** (0.01)	-0.19** (0.08)	0.48*** (0.08)	-0.07*** (0.01)	0.64*** (0.11)	-0.04 (0.06)
BLACK	-0.17*** (0.02)	-0.21* (0.12)	0.49*** (0.10)	-0.002 (0.02)	0.61*** (0.13)	-0.02 (0.08)
OTHERETH	-0.10*** (0.02)	-0.08 (0.12)	0.25* (0.13)	0.06*** (0.02)	0.28 (0.18)	0.06 (0.09)
NORTHE	0.03** (0.01)	0.07 (0.09)	0.10 (0.09)	0.007 (0.01)	0.13 (0.12)	0.01 (0.07)
NORTHW	0.07*** (0.01)	0.05 (0.07)	0.04 (0.09)	0.06*** (0.01)	0.04 (0.12)	0.01 (0.06)
YORKS	-0.04*** (0.01)	-0.10 (0.07)	0.05 (0.09)	-0.06*** (0.01)	0.01 (0.12)	-0.10 (0.06)
EMID	0.06*** (0.01)	-0.02 (0.07)	-0.09 (0.09)	0.002 (0.01)	-0.13 (0.12)	-0.08 (0.07)
WMID	-0.19*** (0.01)	-0.17** (0.07)	0.08 (0.08)	-0.15*** (0.01)	0.07 (0.11)	-0.16* (0.06)
EAST	-0.004 (0.01)	0.01 (0.07)	-0.10 (0.09)	-0.07*** (0.12)	-0.13 (0.12)	-0.07 (0.06)
SOUTHE	-0.07*** (0.01)	-0.09 (0.06)	-0.12 (0.08)	-0.14*** (0.01)	-0.22** (0.11)	-0.18*** (0.06)
SOUTHW	-0.01 (0.01)	0.01 (0.07)	-0.02 (0.09)	-0.06*** (0.01)	-0.03 (0.11)	-0.06 (0.06)
WORKING	-0.09*** (0.01)	-0.13* (0.08)	0.03 (0.09)	-0.16*** (0.01)	-0.04 (0.12)	-0.19*** (0.07)
STUDENT	-0.18*** (0.02)	-0.28** (0.11)	-0.07 (0.16)	-0.16*** (0.02)	-0.21 (0.24)	-0.19* (0.10)
KEEPHOUSE	-0.13*** (0.02)	-0.23** (0.10)	0.38*** (0.12)	-0.10*** (0.02)	0.45*** (0.15)	-0.16* (0.09)
RETIRED	0.25*** (0.02)	0.14 (0.10)	-0.20* (0.11)	0.16*** (0.02)	-0.29* (0.15)	0.11 (0.09)
ILLNOTWORK	-0.42*** (0.03)	-0.58*** (0.14)	0.46*** (0.15)	-0.02 (0.03)	0.45*** (0.19)	-0.11 (0.14)
HE	0.02*** (0.007)	0.11*** (0.04)	-0.31*** (0.05)	-0.02*** (0.007)	-0.39*** (0.06)	0.02 (0.04)
ALEVEL	0.02*** (0.007)	0.001 (0.05)	-0.20*** (0.06)	-0.02*** (0.008)	-0.24*** (0.07)	-0.01 (0.04)
MALE	0.59*** (0.007)	0.56*** (0.04)	-0.33*** (0.05)	0.46*** (0.007)	-0.22*** (0.06)	0.52*** (0.03)
AGE	-0.02*** (0.0003)	-0.026*** (0.002)	0.045*** (0.002)	-0.009*** (0.0003)	0.06*** (0.003)	-0.008*** (0.002)

	(1)	(2)	(3)	(4)	(5)	(6)
DRINKDAILY	0.05*** (0.01)	0.06 (0.06)	−0.10 (0.07)	−0.003 (0.01)	−0.12 (0.09)	0.01 (0.05)
SMKDAILY	0.09*** (0.007)	0.07 (0.04)	0.20*** (0.05)	0.09*** (0.008)	0.32*** (0.07)	0.10*** (0.04)
GENHEALTH	0.27*** (0.004)	0.28*** (0.02)	−0.26*** (0.03)	0.18*** (0.004)	−0.27*** (0.03)	0.19*** (0.02)
NADULT	0.11*** (0.003)	0.09*** (0.02)	−0.05* (0.03)	0.09*** (0.003)	−0.04 (0.04)	0.10*** (0.02)
NCHILD	−0.06*** (0.003)	−0.08*** (0.02)	0.01 (0.02)	−0.08*** (0.004)	−0.003 (0.03)	−0.08*** (0.02)
LOGINCOME	−0.0015 (0.0014)	−0.02** (0.01)	−0.00001 (0.01)	−0.005*** (0.0015)	−0.002 (0.01)	−0.01 (0.008)
SPCLOSE	0.36*** (0.01)	0.43*** (0.08)	−0.55*** (0.09)	0.09*** (0.02)	−0.66*** (0.11)	0.08 (0.08)
VOLUNTARY	0.27*** (0.006)	0.23*** (0.04)	−0.33*** (0.05)	0.15*** (0.006)	−0.36*** (0.06)	0.13*** (0.03)
LIVESPORT	0.20*** (0.007)	0.20*** (0.04)	−0.37*** (0.06)	0.11*** (0.007)	−0.49*** (0.09)	0.12*** (0.04)
TV1HR	−0.07*** (0.01)	−0.13* (0.07)	−0.03 (0.09)	−0.17*** (0.007)	−0.12 (0.12)	−20*** (0.06)
TV2HR	−0.21*** (0.01)	−0.23*** (0.06)	0.07 (0.08)	−0.20*** (0.01)	−0.01 (0.11)	−0.25*** (0.06)
TV3HR	−0.20*** (0.01)	−0.21*** (0.07)	0.19** (0.08)	−0.19*** (0.01)	0.16 (0.11)	−0.22*** (0.06)
TV4HR	−0.30*** (0.01)	−0.32*** (0.07)	0.28*** (0.09)	−0.23*** (0.01)	0.22* (0.12)	−0.30*** (0.07)
TV5PLUS	−0.35*** (0.01)	−0.48*** (0.08)	0.53*** (0.10)	−0.26*** (0.01)	0.53*** (0.13)	−0.33*** (0.07)
TVLIVESPORT	0.25*** (0.007)	0.22*** (0.04)	−0.26*** (0.05)	0.14*** (0.007)	−0.29*** (0.06)	0.129*** (0.04)
TVOTHERSPORT	0.14*** (0.007)	0.15*** (0.04)	−0.27*** (0.05)	0.08*** (0.007)	−0.36*** (0.07)	0.05 (0.04)
CONSTANT	0.62*** (0.15)	1.16 (0.73)	−0.20 (0.71)	2.01*** (012)	−0.80 (0.87)	1.93*** (0.58)
MONTH DUMMIES	YES	YES	YES		YES	
WEIGHTS	YES	YES	N/A		N/A	
Log-likelihood	−132677.78	−37208.99	−81013.58		−33670.67	
Pseudo R²	0.194	0.021				
Number of Iterations	2	4	4		5	
N	12355	12355	12370		12370	

Notes: as Table 2.3.

Table 2.5 Days of participation: alternative count models

Variable	Poisson	Negative Binomial	Zero-inflated Poisson		Zero-inflated Negative Binomial	
			Logit	Poisson	Logit	Neg Bin
SINGLE	−0.06*** (0.02)	−0.10 (0.06)	0.17** (0.07)	−0.01 (0.01)	0.19** (0.08)	−0.02 (0.04)
MARRIED	−0.12*** (0.01)	−0.10* (0.051)	0.08 (0.06)	−0.10*** (0.013)	0.06 (0.07)	−0.12** (0.04)
ASIAN	−0.028 (0.02)	0.01 (0.08)	0.39*** (0.08)	0.08*** (0.02)	0.46*** (0.09)	0.11** (0.05)
BLACK	−0.12*** (0.03)	−0.11 (0.11)	0.52*** (0.10)	0.11*** (0.02)	0.59*** (0.11)	0.12* (0.062)
OTHERETH	−0.22*** (0.03)	−0.15 (0.11)	0.25* (0.13)	0.01 (0.03)	0.26* (0.15)	−0.01 (0.08)
NORTHE	−0.01 (0.02)	0.01 (0.08)	0.17* (0.09)	0.03 (0.02)	0.20** (0.10)	0.04 (0.05)
NORTHW	−0.04** (0.02)	−0.01 (0.06)	0.07 (0.09)	−0.04** (0.02)	0.08 (0.10)	−0.02 (0.05)
YORKS	−0.09*** (0.02)	−0.09 (0.07)	0.06 (0.09)	−0.04** (0.02)	0.06 (0.10)	−0.04 (0.05)
EMID	−0.053*** (0.018)	−0.06 (0.07)	−0.03 (0.09)	−0.048*** (0.02)	−0.05 (0.10)	−0.06 (0.05)
WMID	−0.10*** (0.016)	−0.09 (0.06)	0.08 (0.08)	−0.04* (0.02)	0.09 (0.09)	−0.05 (0.05)
EAST	−0.07*** (0.016)	−0.06 (0.06)	−0.06 (0.09)	−0.07** (0.02)	−0.08 (0.10)	−0.08 (0.05)
SOUTHE	−0.09*** (0.014)	−0.09 (0.06)	−0.09 (0.08)	−0.10*** (0.02)	−0.13 (0.09)	−0.12*** (0.046)
SOUTHW	−0.06*** (0.02)	−0.04 (0.06)	0.02 (0.09)	−0.06*** (0.02)	−0.02 (0.10)	−0.06 (0.05)
WORKING	−0.006 (0.02)	0.01 (0.07)	−0.03 (0.09)	−0.01 (0.02)	−0.05 (0.11)	−0.02 (0.05)
STUDENT	−0.13*** (0.02)	−0.17 (0.11)	−0.08 (0.16)	−0.13*** (0.03)	−0.14 (0.19)	−0.15* (0.08)
KEEPHOUSE	−0.19*** (0.03)	−0.21* (0.10)	0.31*** (0.12)	−0.06** (0.03)	0.33** (0.13)	−0.08 (0.07)
RETIRED	0.13*** (0.03)	0.15 (0.09)	−0.22* (0.12)	0.12*** (0.03)	−0.25* (0.13)	0.13* (0.07)
ILLNOTWORK	−0.299*** (0.04)	−0.21* (0.13)	0.41*** (0.15)	0.10** (0.04)	0.44*** (0.17)	0.124 (0.11)
HE	0.13*** (0.01)	0.16*** (0.04)	−0.29*** (0.05)	0.04*** (0.01)	−0.31*** (0.05)	0.06** (0.03)
ALEVEL	0.06*** (0.01)	0.06 (0.04)	−0.20** (0.06)	0.028*** (0.012)	−0.22*** (0.06)	0.03 (0.03)
MALE	0.18*** (0.01)	0.15 (0.04)	−0.26*** (0.05)	0.08*** (0.01)	−0.25*** (0.05)	0.08*** (0.03)
AGE	−0.02*** (0.0004)	−0.02*** (0.002)	0.041*** (0.002)	−0.003*** (0.0005)	0.05*** (0.003)	−0.003** (0.0013)

	(1)	(2)	(3)	(4)	(5)	(6)
DRINKDAILY	0.07*** (0.01)	0.05 (0.05)	−0.08 (0.07)	−0.01 (0.01)	−0.08 (0.08)	−0.002 (0.04)
SMKDAILY	−0.12*** (0.01)	−0.13*** (0.04)	0.21*** (0.05)	−0.08*** (0.01)	0.22*** (0.06)	−0.08** (0.03)
GENHEALTH	0.172*** (0.006)	0.20*** (0.02)	−0.23*** (0.03)	0.09*** (0.01)	−0.24*** (0.03)	0.095*** (0.016)
NADULT	0.030*** (0.005)	0.02 (0.02)	−0.04 (0.03)	0.02*** (0.005)	−0.04 (0.03)	0.025 (0.02)
NCHILD	−0.027*** (0.005)	−0.04** (0.02)	0.01 (0.02)	−0.03*** (0.005)	0.003 (0.03)	−0.03** (0.014)
LOGINCOME	−0.005** (0.002)	−0.014* (0.008)	0.0004 (0.01)	−0.005*** (0.002)	−0.001 (0.01)	−0.007 (0.006)
SPCLOSE	0.29*** (0.02)	0.37*** (0.07)	−0.53*** (0.09)	0.05*** (0.02)	−0.57*** (0.10)	0.061 (0.06)
VOLUNTARY	0.19*** (0.01)	0.18*** (0.04)	−0.32*** (0.05)	0.05*** (0.009)	−0.34*** (0.05)	0.056* (0.026)
LIVESPORT	0.132*** (0.01)	0.14** (0.04)	−0.33*** (0.06)	0.05*** (0.01)	−0.37*** (0.07)	0.055** (0.03)
TV1HR	−0.04** (0.02)	−0.08 (0.07)	−0.04 (0.09)	−0.06*** (0.02)	−0.06 (0.10)	−0.07 (0.05)
TV2HR	−0.13*** (0.01)	−0.13** (0.06)	0.06 (0.08)	−0.07*** (0.02)	0.05 (0.09)	−0.077* (0.04)
TV3HR	−0.17*** (0.02)	−0.18*** (0.06)	0.18** (0.08)	−0.07*** (0.02)	0.17* (0.10)	−0.08* (0.05)
TV4HR	−0.284*** (0.02)	−0.26*** (0.07)	0.28*** (0.09)	−0.11*** (0.02)	0.27* (0.10)	−0.126*** (0.05)
TV5PLUS	−0.38*** (0.02)	−0.42*** (0.08)	0.51*** (0.10)	−0.12*** (0.02)	0.53*** (0.11)	−0.125** (0.06)
TVLIVESPORT	0.14*** (0.01)	0.127*** (0.04)	−0.23*** (0.05)	0.04*** (0.01)	−0.24*** (0.05)	0.05 (0.03)
TVOTHERSPORT	0.15*** (0.01)	0.16*** (0.04)	−0.28*** (0.05)	0.03*** (0.01)	−0.32*** (0.06)	0.022 (0.03)
CONSTANT	1.43*** (0.16)	1.64** (0.65)	−0.64 (0.72)	2.21*** (0.13)	−0.87 (0.79)	2.18*** (0.40)
MONTH DUMMIES	YES	YES	YES		YES	
WEIGHTS	YES	YES	N/A		N/A	
Log-likelihood	−61255.07	−30473.77	−37160.22		−27653.01	
Pseudo R²	0.09	0.01				
Number of Iterations	2	3	3		4	
N	11632	11632	11645		11645	

Notes: as Table 2.3.

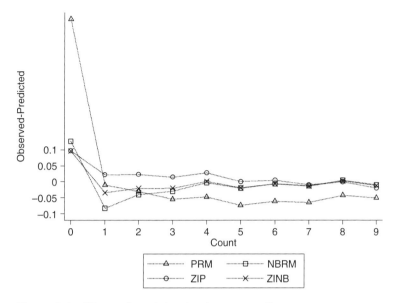

Figure 2.4   Hours of participation (aggregated)

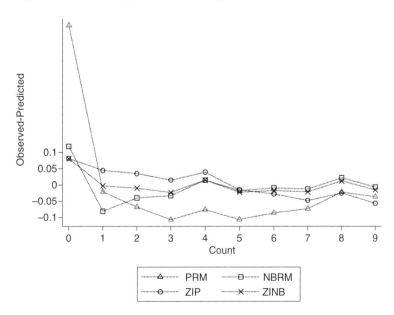

Figure 2.5   Days of participation (aggregated)

Table 2.6   Comparison of count models – test statistics

Hours of Participation				
	Poisson	**Neg Bin**	**ZIP**	**ZINB**
AIC	20.02	5.59	13.12	5.46
BIC	131 426.2	−46 997.7	46 425.4	−48 250.96
Likelihood Ratio Test		[a]1.78 x 10^5		[b]94 685.81
Vuong Test			[c]51.70	[d]26.61
Days of Participation				
	Poisson	**Neg Bin**	**ZIP**	**ZINB**
AIC	10.39	4.97	6.40	4.77
BIC	12 347.17	50 792.86	33 752.42	−52 757.48
Likelihood Ratio Test		[a]63 149.39		[b]19 014.43
Vuong Test			[c]55.89	[d]27.74

Notes:
a   Likelihood ratio test of Poisson vs negative binomial.
b   Likelihood ratio test of ZIP vs ZINB.
c   Non-nested Vuong test of Poisson vs ZIP.
d   Non-nested Vuong test of negative binomial vs ZINB.

estimated count models. The plots reveal that the Poisson model under-predicts the number of zeros by a large margin. The NBR model does better but it appears that the zero-inflated models perform best.

A number of formal statistics were used to make direct comparisons of the count models (Table 2.6). The likelihood ratio test of over-dispersion indicates that the NBR is favoured over the Poisson in both the hours and days participation equations. The non-nested Vuong test confirms the appropriateness of zero-inflated models over the Poisson and NBR counterparts. Comparisons between Poisson and ZINB and NBR and ZIP are made using the Akaike Information Criterion (AIC) and Bayesian Information Criterion (BIC). Overall, the results suggest that the ZINB is the preferred model, and this is consistent with the prior expectations about the data noted earlier.

DISCUSSION AND CONCLUDING REMARKS

As far as the authors can discern, the above results constitute the first analysis of the relationship between the demands for participation sport and sport watched either live or via the media. The research is important because it provides an opportunity to comment upon current sports policy in the UK, which, particularly in the case of the Olympic Games, makes a case that watching live sport or sport on the broadcast media might encourage participation and thus consequently contribute to the well-being and health of the nation. Significantly too, governing bodies and community sports policy emanating from Sport England is concerned with promoting sports participation to underpin elite sports development and to contribute to the development of specific sports as a contribution to the health and well-being of the nation.

Naturally the results on many of the covariates are as expected. Being male, younger, unmarried and broadly white British promotes sports participation, as does education. The presence of children in the household and lifestyle factors such as smoking reduce participation. Of most significance to this chapter, however, is that a broad complementarity is identified between sports participation and viewing sports either live or via the media as live or recorded activities. Naturally this provides support for the current emphasis of sports policy in the UK. However, these remarks should be tempered by the general broad finding that increased TV watching hours is linked to reduced participation.

This suggests some potential refinements of emphasis for policy makers. As Downward and Rasciute (2010) find, there is evidence of substitution effects in the UK between sports and leisure activities. The current research suggests likewise for the most common of leisure pursuits. Consequently, in as much that promoting further sport on TV adds to total TV viewing, this suggests potential adverse consequences on participation. Clearly the impact of these interactions needs to be unpicked further. One particularly important line of future enquiry should be to try to identify the causality between sport viewing in the media and general TV viewing. However, in as much that attending sports events live is complementary to participation, there is the suggestion that participation and sports spectatorship generally are manifestations of a latent variable of 'sport' consumption. In this respect, policy may be better targeted at promoting this more general consumer activity than focusing on its constituent parts per se.

ACKNOWLEDGEMENTS

An earlier version of this paper was presented at the First European Conference in Sports Economics, held at University Paris 1 Panthéon Sorbonne, 14–15 September 2009. We are grateful for comments received at the conference.

NOTES

1. The development and origin of professional sports and their tournaments is discussed further in Downward *et al.* (2009). Suffice it to note in the current context that in the UK, the now traditional knockout cup competitions were typically the original basis of competition, but as the sports developed and embraced professionalism, leagues, that is round-robin tournaments, developed. These have now further evolved to accommodate multi-stage tournaments such as playoffs and international competitions such as the Champions League and Heineken Cup.
2. A careful distinction is drawn between the levels of economic activity and significance of the events and their impact. It is only in the latter case that the net benefits of sports events are identified. The evidence is that these impacts are likely to be weak (see Baade, 2007).
3. It should be noted that the distinction between public and private sector activity is blurred in the UK. Some private sector businesses have been harnessed to underwrite public sector policy projects in conjunction with governing bodies. For example McDonald's sponsors community football activities for the FA, whilst David Lloyd Leisure hosts Lawn Tennis Association activities, and so on. Moreover, previously public sector leisure centres are now run by franchised private sector organizations since Compulsory Competitive Tendering and Best Value were introduced to the provision of public sector services in the 1980s and 1990s respectively.
4. These are interesting findings, but one potential problem with these results, which are derived from two separate regressions controlling for the impact of each alternative viewing option, is that other intervening factors could influence the broadcasting demand equation, such as the attractiveness of the fixture. In other words, only aggregate results can be generated. In this research, data on the same individuals can be examined.
5. At the time of writing, the second and third years of the survey are yet to be made publically available.
6. In the initial stages of the data analysis, it became apparent that for a small number of observations, the number of minutes, hours and days of participation exceeded the maximum possible. In the case of number of minutes, for example, one individual's total exceeded 40 320, which is based on participation in sport for 24 hours a day for the four-week period. Limiting the maximum to the more

realistic case of 8 hours or 12 hours per day leads to a reduction of 29 and 14 observations respectively.

7. The reduced sample size refers to the 'core' of observations across the covariates in which missing values were deleted to facilitate comparison of models. Where necessary, weights were attached to the estimators to control for the sampling biases in the dataset.

8. Given the similarity between hours and minutes, we do not include analysis relating to minutes of participation from this point onwards.

REFERENCES

Alavy, K., Gaskell, A., Leach, S. and Szymanski, S. (2006), *On the Edge of Your Seat: Demand for Football on Television and the Uncertainty of Outcome Hypothesis*, International Association of Sports Economists Working Paper 06-31, Limoges: IASE.

Baade, R. (2007), 'The Economic Impact of Mega-Sporting Events', in W. Andreff and S. Szymanski (eds), *The Handbook of the Economics of Sport*, Cheltenham, UK: Edward Elgar Publishing, pp. 177–182.

Baimbridge, M., Cameron, S. and Dawson, P. (1996), 'Satellite Broadcasting and the Demand for Football: A Whole New Ball Game?' *Scottish Journal of Political Economy*, **43**, 317–333.

Borland, J. and MacDonald, R. (2003), 'Demand for Sport', *Oxford Review of Economic Policy*, **19**, 478–502.

Buraimo, B. (2008), 'Stadium Attendance and Television Audience Demand in English League Football', *Managerial and Decision Economics*, **29**, 513–523.

Cameron, A.C. and Trivedi, P.K. (2005), *Microeconometrics: Methods and Applications*, New York: Cambridge University Press.

Campbell, R.M. Jr, Aiken, D. and Kent, A. (2004), 'Beyond BIRGing and CORFing: Continuing the Exploration of Fan Behavior', *Sport Marketing Quarterly*, **13**, 151–157.

Clowes, J. and Tapp, A. (2003), 'Looking Through the Hourglass of Fan Segmentation: Research Findings and Marketing Implications for Live Spectator Sports', *International Journal of Sports Marketing and Sponsorship*, **5**, 57–73.

Crawford, G. (2003), 'The Career of the Sport Supporter: The Case of the Manchester Storm' *Sociology*, **37**, 219–237.

Crompton, J. (1995), 'Economic Impact Analysis of Sports Facilities and Events: Eleven Sources of Misapplication', *Journal of Sports Management*, **9**, 14–35.

Crompton, J. (2006), 'Economic Impact Studies: Instruments for Political Shenanigans?' *Journal of Travel Research*, **45**, 67–82.

DCMS (2008), *Playing to Win: A New Era For Sport*, London: DCMS.

DCMS/Strategy Unit (2002), *Game Plan: A Strategy for Delivering Government's Sport and Physical Activity Objectives*, London: DCMS.

Downward, P.M., Dawson, A. and Dejonghe, T. (2009), *Sports Economics: Theory, Evidence and Policy*, London: Butterworth-Heinemann.

Downward, P.M. and Rasciute, S. (2010), 'The Relative Demands for Sport and Leisure in England', *European Sport Management Quarterly*, **10** (2), 189–214.

Downward, P.M. and Riordan, J. (2007), 'Social Interactions and the Demand for Sport: An Economic Analysis', *Contemporary Economic Policy*, **25**, 518–537.

Forrest, D., Simmons, R. and Buraimo, B. (2005), 'Outcome Uncertainty and the Couch Potato Audience', *Scottish Journal of Political Economy*, **52**, 641–661.

Forrest, D., Simmons, R. and Szymanski, S. (2004), 'Broadcasting, Attendance and the Inefficiency of Cartels', *Review of Industrial Organization*, **24**, 243–265.

Funk, D.C. and James, J.D. (2001), 'The Psychological Continuum Model (PCM): A Conceptual Framework for Understanding an Individual's Psychological Connection to Sport', *Sport Management Review*, **4**, 119–150.

Giulianotti, R. (1995), 'Football, Violence and Social Identity', *The Editorial Board of the Sociological Review*, s213–217.

Glyptis, S. (1982), *Sport and Tourism in Western Europe*, London: British Travel Education Trust.

Gratton, C. and Taylor, P. (2000), *The Economics of Sport and Recreation*, London: Spon.

Greene, W. (2008), *Econometric Analysis* (6th edn), London: Prentice Hall.

Heckman, J.J. (1979), 'Sample Selection Bias as a Specification Error', *Econometrica*, **47**, 153–161.

Humphreys, B. and Ruseski, J. (2006), *Economic Determinants of Participation in Physical Activity and Sport*, IASE Working Papers, 06-13, Limoges, International Association of Sports Economists.

Hunt, K.A., Bristol, T. and Bashaw, E.R. (1999), 'A Conceptual Approach to Classifying Sports Fans', *Journal of Services Marketing*, **13**, 439–452.

Késenne, S. (1981), 'Time-Allocation and the Linear Expenditure System', *Recherches Economiques de Louvain*, **46**, 113–125.

Késenne, S. (1983), 'Substitution in Consumption: An Application to the Allocation of Time', *European Economic Review*, **23**, 231–239.

Késenne, S. and Butzen, P. (1987), 'Subsidising Sports Facilities: The Shadow Price-Elasticities of Sports', *Applied Economics*, **19**, 101–110.

Lera-López, F. and Rapún-Gárate, M. (2005), 'Sports Participation versus Consumer Expenditure on Sport: Different Determinants and Strategies in Sports Management', *European Sports Management Quarterly*, **5**, 167–186.

Mahony, D.F., Madrigal, R. and Howard, D.R. (2000), 'Using the Psychological Commitment to Team (PCT) Scale to Segment Sport Consumers Based on Loyalty', *Sport Marketing Quarterly*, **9**, 15–25.

Mullahy, J. (1986), 'Specification and Testing of some Modified Count Models', *Journal of Econometrics*, **33**, 341–365.

Preuss, H. (2004), *The Economics of Staging the Olympics: A Comparison of the Games 1972–2008*, Cheltenham: Edward Elgar.

Stewart B., Smith, A. and Nicholson, M. (2003), 'Sport Consumer Typologies: A Critical Review', *Sport Marketing Quarterly*, **12**, 206–216.

Stratton, M., Conn, L., Liaw, C. and Connolly, L. (2005), 'Sport and Related Physical Activity: The Social Correlates of Participation and Non-Participation by Adults', paper presented at the *Sport Management Association of Australia and New Zealand Conference*, Canberra.

Taks, M. and Scheerder, J. (2006), 'Youth Sports Participation Styles and Market Segmentation Profiles: Evidence and Applications', *European Sport Management Quarterly*, **6**, 85–121.

Trail, G., Anderson, D. and Fink, J. (2000), 'A Theoretical Model of Sport Spectator Consumption Behaviour', *International Journal of Sport Management*, **3**, 154–180.

Trail, G., Fink, J. and Anderson, D. (2003), 'Sport Spectator Consumption Behavior', *Sport Marketing Quarterly*, **12**, 8–17.

Vuong, Q. (1989), 'Likelihood Ratio Tests for Model Selection and Non-Nested Hypotheses', *Econometrica*, **57**, 307–333.

Weed, M. and Bull, C. (2004), *Sports Tourism: Participants, Policy and Providers*, London: Butterworth Heinemann.

Wicker, P., Breuer, C. and Pawlowski, T. (2009), 'Promoting Sport for All to Age-Specific Target Groups: The Impact of Sport Infrastructure', *European Sports Management Quarterly*, **9**, 103–118.

Wooldridge, J. (2002), *Econometric Analysis of Cross Section and Panel Data*, Boston, MA: MIT Press.

3. Relational goods at work! Crime and sport participation in Italy: evidence from panel data regional analysis over the period 1997–2003

Raul Caruso

INTRODUCTION

The conventional wisdom about sport participation takes for granted that a beneficial impact of sport on society is predictable. The Commission of the European Union, for example, in 2007 released a White Paper on sport which emphasizes the beneficial impact of sport on society.[1] The White Paper defines 'sport' as 'all forms of physical activity which, through casual or organised participation, aim at expressing or improving physical fitness and mental well-being, forming social relationships or obtaining results in competition at all levels'. The White Paper highlights some specific benefits: (i) public health through physical activity; (ii) reinforcement of human capital thanks to development of knowledge, motivation, skills and readiness for personal effort; and (iii) active citizenship, social inclusion and integration. In brief, sport seems to enhance both individual and social well-being. However, the White Paper also highlights the importance and peculiarities of the professional sport industry, so stressing also the direct positive impact of sport on economic growth. Clearly, the White Paper rests to a large extent upon the conventional idea that sport is beneficial for society.

However, this is a modern idea. In ancient and medieval societies, for example, sport was considered the peacetime occupation of the nobles, whose main business was war. Sport participation was not interpreted as enjoyment or leisure. It was ancillary to the training for war. This example clarifies why I am concerned with the modern conventional point of view. However, I do not want necessarily to propose a different way of thinking. I only want to highlight some points we might consider in order to better evaluate the societal role of sport participation. In fact, the aim of this chapter is to study empirically whether or not there is a relationship between sport participation and crime. That is, the approach here is that of studying the potential benefits of sport participation indirectly; it is assumed that fewer (or less intense) pernicious factors can lead to more desirable social outcomes. Hence, I assume henceforth that a social outcome exhibiting fewer crimes must be preferred to a social outcome characterized by a higher level of crime. Hence, in this respect, the impact of sport participation on crime is expected to be negative.

However, such association is not clear when considering different types of crime. In some cases, for example, juvenile crime and violence emerge in the presence of juvenile groups clustered around sport participation identity. Narratives of hooliganism sadly confirm this. Moreover, other studies have indicated positive associations between sports and anti-social behaviour. For example, young athletes have higher levels of drug and alcohol use (Ewing, 1998b; Overman and Terry, 1991), binge drinking and an increased tendency to be involved in physical fights than non-athletes (Endresen and Olweus, 2005; Rutten *et al.*, 2007). Therefore, these simple examples show how the broad question still remains largely unanswered. What is the broad impact of sport participation and sport activities in a society?

The chapter can be split into two parts. In the first part, I propose a novel economic definition of sport participation. Sport is defined as a good with a multiple nature which combines components of: (i) exchange; (ii) coercion; and (iii) integrative relationships. In the second section, by means of panel data of Italian regions, I analyse the impact of sport participation on the rate of: (i) property crimes; (ii) violent crime; and (iii) juvenile crime. Finally, a summary of findings is presented.

THE ECONOMIC NATURE OF SPORT PARTICIPATION

Before analysing in depth the relationship between sport partici-pation and crime, we need an economic definition of sport. Such a definition should encompass the multiple and multifaceted aspects of sport participation. The multiple dimensions of sport participation can be interpreted following the theoretical approach expounded by British economist Kenneth Boulding (see Boulding, 1963, 1968, 1973, 1978). To Boulding, the social system can be divided into three large, overlapping and interacting sub-systems: (i) exchange, (ii) threat; and (iii) integrative systems.[2] All human interactions involve different combinations of all three components. Exchange relationships consti-tute the usual domain of economics. In its simplest form, two parties agree to exchange something with something else, usually money with goods and services. The threat system is a relationship between two parties in which one party is capable of affecting the behaviour of the other through coercion. The threat system is less productive than the exchange system simply because the exchange of goods encourages the production of more goods, whereas threat discourages the pro-duction of goods. A threat system is intrinsically unproductive and unstable in the long run. Thirdly, an integrative relationship takes shape in the presence of: (i) an interdependence of utility functions of the parties involved; and (ii) unilateral transfers between agents. Classical examples are gift giving, charity donations and family re-lationships. Integrative systems are directly linked with the very fabric of human sociality because they also involve a complex spectrum of feelings, such as respect, love, affection and so on. To Boulding, inte-grative systems sustain the stable development of societies.

With regard to the 'exchange' component within sport, this is the domain of classical sport economics, which has been expand-ing recently, and whose founding pillars are Rottenberg (1956) and Neale (1964). Comprehensive accounts are Fort and Quirk (1995), Szymanski (2003), Zimbalist (2003) and Andreff (2008), and a novel interpretation in the light of the theory of multi-sided markets can be found in Budzinski and Satzer (2008).

With regard to the integrative dimension of sport, it is possible to refer to the emerging theory of relational goods, which fits perfectly with Boulding's approach of integrative systems. It contributes to an explanation of the shaping of human sociality.[3] The theory of relational goods has been developed in Ulhaner (1989), Gui (2000), Bruni (2006) and Bruni and Stanca (2006). Relational goods 'depend upon interactions among persons' (Ulhaner, 1989, p. 253) and are peculiarly 'intangible outputs of an affective and communicative nature' (Gui 2000) that are produced through social interactions. The relational good is the relationship in itself. Hence, relational goods are non-rival. Secondly, relational goods are simultaneously produced and consumed. Eventually, motivations of agents matter. Hence, the expected value of relational goods will depend upon the traits, inclinations and motivations of the agents involved. In the end, a relational good cannot be anonymous. In fact, a relational good produced and consumed by agents A and B at a particular time and place differs from a relational good produced by agents C and D at a different place or time. Suppose for simplicity that A=C and B=D. Even in this case, a relational good produced and consumed by A and B differs from a good produced by A and B in either a different place or time. For our purposes, take the example of a sport activity. If two friends, Ivan and Jacob, play tennis every day, the relational good – 'tennis match' – takes a different shape every day. The Monday match will be different from the Tuesday match and so on. Needless to say, a match played by Ivan and Jacob will be different from a match played between John and Jimmy. In brief, a relational good must necessarily be a *named* good in the spirit of Hahn (1971).

With regard to the third component of the current approach, in many cases, sport participation is by no means a pure expression of voluntary choice. It can involve threat, coercion, aggressive behaviour and extreme competition. In the eyes of the economist, these behaviours are intrinsically unproductive or even destructive. To explain this point, consider some historical examples. The Soviet Union constitutes a good example in this respect. In fact, since the end of World War II, the East European (and world communist) sports system has been dominated by clubs in the security forces and armed forces. Most sport heroes have officially been soldiers or police officers, guardians of public order and role models for a disciplined, obedient and patriotic citizenry. Thus, to many people, sport, has been identified in the popular consciousness with paramilitary coercion (Riordan, 1993). Sport participation was an element of a broader mechanism designed to fully control the society (Howell, 1975; Cooper, 1989). Moreover, the sport system was also interpreted as an ancillary to foreign policy. In fact, success in sport helped the

USSR, East Germany, Cuba and other socialist countries to gain international recognition and prestige (Riordan, 1974). Nowadays, this phenomenon is still pervasive in many autocracies. However, unfortunately there are examples of sporting clubs directly managed by security forces in the western democracies too. Such intertwining between sports and the military dates back to past ages. As noted above, in ancient and medieval societies, sport was considered the peacetime occupation of the nobles, whose main business was war (Carter, 1985). Moreover, Cornell and Allen (2002), in a brilliant collective book, deepen the close connection between war and games in different ages. In sum, sport participation was not presented as enjoyment or leisure but as descending from men's warring attitudes.

The multiple definition of sport participation envisioned above implies that the social outcome of sport participation would depend on the intensity of the different elements. In developing this point, I assume that the relational and integrative intensity of sport participation must necessarily be positive, whilst the threat and exchange elements can perhaps exhibit a null intensity. This leads to the following economic definition of sport as:

> a joint indivisible good, which is produced and consumed by different agents at a certain place and time. It retains a multiple nature. In fact, it is a combination of: (i) a market good, (ii) a relational good and (iii) an expression of threat, power and coercion. All components differ in intensity, but differently from (i) and (iii) the relational component must necessarily be positive.

Such a definition encompasses the three components highlighted in Boulding's theory of social interactions. Therefore, finally, given such a definition, we can propose the following hypothesis: 'Sport may be beneficial for society as long as the relational component dominates both the coercive and the exchange components'.

How might such a hypothesis be defended? First, we can refer to the growing empirical literature on the impact of relational goods. A positive correlation between the happiness of individuals and relational goods is commonly recognized. Becchetti *et al.* (2006, 2008) show that relational goods have significant and positive effects on self-declared life satisfaction. Forrest and McHale (2009) also explore the relationship between self-reported happiness and sport participation. Results indicate that women who choose to play sport increase their well-being compared to women with similar demographic and socio-economic characteristics by an amount which is substantive and statistically significant. However, the same result does not emerge for males.

Lechner (2009), using data from the German Socio-Economic Panel Study (GSOEP) from 1984 to 2006, analyses the impact of sport participation on subjective well-being. Three measures of well-being are used: (i) being worried about the economic situation; (ii) general satisfaction with life; and (iii) general satisfaction with health. The results show that sport participation is beneficial for subjective well-being. The study also reports a positive association between sport participation and earnings in the long run. The latter finding, in particular, has been investigated several times in the US. Henderson, Olbrecht and Polachek (2006) established that the wage distribution of former college athletes is different from that of non-athletes, and that sport participation constitutes a significant determinant of wages. By means of non-parametric regression, the authors show that former athletes earn a wage premium which varies across occupations. This is consistent with previous empirical evidence. Long and Caudill (1991) show that males who participated in college athletics were estimated to earn more than individuals who did not participate in any athletic activity. In particular, former male athletes have been estimated to earn 4 per cent more than former non-athletes. However, there is no similar evidence for females. The sample is made up of almost ten thousand individuals in the early stages of their careers in 1980 who attended college in the early 1970s.

Ewing (1998a) found that high school athletes are likely to be associated with better labour outcomes than non-athletes. The sample of the study is 1301 individuals, of whom 55 per cent participated in high school athletics. Three measures of work attainment are used: (i) performance-based pay; (ii) union membership; and (iii) the number of workers supervised by the respondent. By means of logistic estimators, the author shows that former athletes exhibit better labour outcomes. Ewing (2007) extends the previous work. The sample consists of 1782 individuals. Twenty per cent of the respondents actively participated in high school athletics. It is confirmed that these individuals perform better in terms of both components of the compensation structure (wages and fringe benefits) than non-athletes. Therefore, it appears that sport participation implies positive monetary and non-monetary benefits for individuals. This can produce beneficial spillovers to the whole society. In the next section, I present the core analysis of this study, namely the empirical investigation on the association between sport participation and crime, which is assumed to be a significant proxy for evaluating a social outcome.

DATA AND EMPIRICAL EVIDENCE

Next, I present an empirical investigation on the association between sport participation and three types of crime: (i) property crime; (ii) violent crime; and (iii) juvenile crime. Property crimes consist of thefts, robberies and burglaries. In particular, the property crime rate is computed as the ratio of property crimes over the total number of crimes. Violent crimes are rapes, homicides, kidnappings, injuries and lesions. The index of violent crime is computed as the rate of violent crime per ten thousand inhabitants. Juvenile crime includes every crime committed by young people below the age of 18. The index of juvenile crime is computed as the percentage ratio of crimes committed by young people to the total number of crimes. Table 3.1 reports descriptive statistics of the variables used. All data come from the Italian National Statistical Office (ISTAT). All figures are collected on a regional basis. Italian administrative regions correspond to NUTS II level.

The results are reported in Tables 3.2, 3.3 and 3.4. In Table 3.2, the dependent variable is the rate of property crime. In this table,

Table 3.1   Descriptive statistics

Variables (Logged)	Obs.	Mean	St. Dev.	Min	Max
Property crime	140	4.02	0.181	3.22	4.33
Violent crime	140	2.33	0.359	1.16	3.41
Juvenile crime	140	0.96	0.305	0.095	1.67
Sport participation	140	3.34	0.252	2.83	3.87
Unemployment	140	2.18	0.596	0.9	3.2
Unemployment (one year lagged)	140	2.23	0.569	0.9	3.2
GDP per capita	140	9.71	0.317	7.6	10.1
Literacy	140	4.22	0.103	3.92	4.42
Security	140	6.48	1.069	3.7	8
Social protection	140	5.38	0.998	3.24	7.49

Source: ISTAT, 1997–2003.

Table 3.2   Results: sport participation and crime in Italy 1997–2003 (property)

				OLS fixed effects				
	(1)	(2)	(3)	(4)	(5)	(6)	(7)	(8)
Sport	**−0.45***	**−0.30***	**−0.29***	**−0.24**	**−0.30***			**−0.27**
	(0.10)	(0.05)	(0.11)	(0.11)	(0.11)			(0.12)
	[0.00]	[0.01]	[0.01]	[0.03]	[0.01]			[0.03]
GDP per capita					0.00	0.01		
					(0.04)	(0.04)		
					[0.91]	[0.84]		
(Sport × Literacy)						**−0.05***		
						(0.02)		
						[0.01]		
(Sport × GDP per capita)							−0.01	
							(0.01)	
							[0.18]	
Unemployment			0.01					
			(0.05)					
			[0.84]					
Lagged unemployment (t−1)		**0.14***	**0.13**		**0.14***	**0.12**	**0.16***	0.01
		(0.11)	(0.06)		(0.05)	(0.06)	(0.05)	(0.07)
		[0.01]	[0.05]		[0.01]	[0.04]	[0.00]	[0.90]

	(1)	(2)	(3)	(4)	(5)	(6)	(7)	(8)
Literacy							-0.14 (0.18) [0.45]	0.13 (0.19) [0.51]
Security				0.45 (0.28) [0.11]				
Social protection				-0.43*** (0.11) [0.00]				-0.37*** (0.14) [0.01]
constant	5.53*** (0.33) [0.00]	4.7*** (0.44) [0.00]	4.68*** (0.45) [0.00]	4.2*** (1.62) [0.01]	4.7*** (0.53) [0.00]	4.44*** (0.48) [0.00]	4.62*** (0.78) [0.00]	6.34*** (0.95) [0.00]
Obs	140	140	140	140	140	140	140	140
Groups	20	20	20	20	20	20	20	20
R² within	0.15	0.2	0.2	0.25	0.20	0.2	0.18	0.24
R² between	0.36	0.3	0.3	0.16	0.29	0.25	0.21	0.57
R² overall	0.22	0.17	0.17	0.09	0.17	0.14	0.12	0.42

Notes:
Standard errors in parentheses. P-values in square brackets. Significant coefficients in bold: *** 1%, ** 5%, * 10%.
Dependent variable: index of property crime (ratio of property crimes over the total number of crimes).

51

Table 3.3 Results: sport participation and crime in Italy 1997–2003 (violence)

	OLS fixed effects							
	(1)	(2)	(3)	(4)	(5)	(6)	(7)	(8)
Sport	0.42*** (0.15) [0.00]	0.27* (0.17) [0.11]	0.31* (0.19) [0.10]		0.30* −0.18 [0.10]		0.26 (0.19) [0.18]	0.26 (0.17) [0.13]
GDP per capita			0.02 (0.06) [0.99]		0.02 (0.06) [0.78]	0.01 (0.06) [0.83]		0.18 (0.06) [0.75]
(Sport × Literacy)						0.06* (0.03) [0.08]		
(Sport × GDP per capita)				0.02* (0.11) [0.08]				
Lagged unemployment (t − 1)		−0.13* (0.08) [0.08]			−1.19* (0.11) [0.10]	−0.18* (0.11) [0.11]	−0.18* (0.11) [0.11]	−0.13* (0.08) [0.08]
Literacy			0.16 (0.27) [0.58]				0.15 (0.3) [0.61]	

	(1)	(2)	(3)	(4)	(5)	(6)	(7)	(8)
Security	0.92* (0.5) [0.07]	1.72*** (0.67) [0.01]	0.37 (0.41) [0.36]	0.53 (0.39) [0.17]	0.29 (0.46) [0.52]	0.28 (0.23) [0.27]	0.3 (0.45) [0.51]	
Social protection					-0.2 (0.22) [0.37]	-0.25 (0.23) [0.27]	-0.24 (0.24) [0.31]	
constant			-1.79 (2.47) [0.47]	-1.79 (2.44) [0.47]	0.77 (2.96) [0.79]	1.3 (2.91) [0.66]	0.54 (3.00) [0.86]	1.58** (0.81) [0.05]
Obs	140	140	140	140	140	140	140	140
Groups	20	20	20	20	20	20	20	20
R^2 within	0.06	0.09	0.08	0.09	0.1	0.1	0.1	0.09
R^2 between	0.38	0.39	0.39	0.08	0.04	0.09	0.01	0.04
R^2 overall	0.34	0.34	0.35	0.04	0.04	0.09	0.01	0.02

Notes:
Standard errors in parentheses. P-values in square brackets. Significant coefficients in bold: *** 1%, ** 5%, * 10%.
Dependent variable: index of violent crime (rate of violent crime per ten thousand inhabitants).

Table 3.4 Results: sport participation and crime in Italy 1997–2003 (juvenile crime)

	OLS fixed effects							
	(1)	(2)	(3)	(4)	(5)	(6)	(7)	(8)
Sport	**−0.81*****	**−0.5***	**−0.8*****	**−0.8*****				−0.16
	(0.25)	(0.29)	(0.26)	(0.27)				(0.32)
	[0.00]	[0.09]	[0.00]	[0.00]				[0.61]
GDP per capita			−0.04	−0.04	−0.03	−0.06		
			(0.10)	(0.10)	(0.10)	(0.10)		
			[0.71]	[0.71]	[0.78]	[0.52]		
(Sport × Literacy)					**−0.18*****	**−0.13*****		
					(0.45)	(0.05)		
					[0.00]	[0.02]		
(Sport × GDP per capita)							−0.02	
							(0.02)	
							[0.45]	
Lagged unemployment (*t*−1)		**0.27****				**0.26***	**0.23***	0.15
		(0.13)				(0.15)	(0.14)	(0.14)
		[0.03]				[0.08]	[0.10]	[0.28]
Literacy							**−1.11*****	**−1.06*****
							(0.45)	(0.46)
							[0.01]	[0.02]

54

	(1)	(2)	(3)	(4)	(5)	(6)	(7)	(8)
Security	3.67***	2.00*		-0.06	0.35	0.85	0.95	
	(0.85)	(1.14)		(0.66)	(0.67)	(0.72)	(4.91)	
	[0.00]	[0.08]		[0.92]	[0.60]	[0.24]	[0.91]	
constant			3.99***	4.35	1.45	-2.7	-0.53	5.67***
			(1.21)	(4.2)	(4.2)	(4.8)	(4.91)	(1.94)
			[0.00]	[0.30]	[0.73]	[0.57]	[0.91]	[0.00]
Obs	140	140	140	140	140	140	140	140
Groups	20	20	20	20	20	20	20	20
R² within	0.08	0.11	0.09	0.08	0.13	0.15	0.16	0.15
R² between	0.52	0.39	0.49	0.49	0.08	0.03	0.01	0.12
R² overall	0.22	0.16	0.21	0.21	0.03	0.01	0.00	0.02

Notes:
Standard errors in parentheses. P-values in square brackets. Significant coefficients in bold: *** 1%, ** 5%, * 10%.
Dependent variable: index of juvenile crime (percentage ratio of crimes committed by young individuals to the total number of crimes).

the main finding is that sport participation significantly reduces the level of property crime. In Table 3.3, the dependent variable is the rate of violent crime. It is shown that sport participation is positively associated with the incidence of violent crime, but the evidence is only weakly significant. In Table 3.4, the dependent variable is the rate of juvenile crime defined as the percentage of crimes committed by minors (<18 years old) on the total number of crimes. Sport participation is negatively associated with juvenile crime.

In all tables, the first column reports the simplest baseline model. The dependent variable is regressed only on the sport participation rate. At the same time, I also investigate eight different specifications. In Table 3.2, in all of them the association between property crime and sport participation is negative and highly significant. In Table 3.3, the results show a positive association between violent crime and sport participation. In Table 3.4, all further specifications confirm a negative association between sport participation and juvenile crime.

In all specifications, the lagged unemployment rate has been used as covariate. There is an established literature which has analysed the impact of unemployment on crime rates (see among others Burdett *et al.*, 2003 and Britt, 1997). In general, criminologists and other social scientists have often been interested in the relationship between crime and economic development. In fact, unemployment is often considered as a proxy of general economic conditions. It is expected to capture the opportunity cost of committing crimes. Even GDP per capita is frequently assumed to be a measure of social well-being. However, it can be misleading. First, GDP per capita may measure aggregate economic activity and not social well-being. Second, GDP measures only current economic activity but says little about future economic scenarios. By contrast, individuals take into account current as well as future conditions. This is particularly important when considering crime. As Campiglio (1990) pointed out, the rate of unemployment captures the expected difference in returns between legal and illegal activities. The higher the rate of unemployment, the smaller is this difference. Therefore, the opportunity cost of committing crime is lower. In particular, Scorcu and Cellini (1998) show how the long-term trend of property crimes is associated with unemployment in Italy over the period 1951–1994. The specification also follows the intuition expounded in Levitt (2001), which includes both the current unemployment rate and lagged unemployment rates. Following this intuition, the choice of committing a crime depends on both current and past income. Finally, in Table 3.2, lagged unemployment is significantly associated with crime rates in specifications 2, 3, 5, 6, and 7. In Table 3.3, it seems to be negatively associated with violent crime but the association is weakly significant. In Table 3.4, lagged unemployment is positively associated with juvenile crime. In particular, the association is more robust in column 2, where the specification is more parsimonious. GDP per capita has also been included as covariate in all the tables. It does not show any significant association with crime rates.

Surprisingly, public spending on security seems to be ineffective in all specifications. In other words, it seems that deterrence has no role in preventing or reducing crime. However, this confirms the results presented in Caruso (2009a) for organized crime in Italy. Moreover, in all tables, the association between types of crime and literacy is not conclusive. In Tables 3.2 and 3.3, there is no significant association between crime and literacy, but in Table 3.4, the association between juvenile crime and sport participation is negative and highly significant. However, it is interesting to note that the interaction term between sport participation and literacy (sport × literacy) shows a significant negative association in Tables 3.2 and 3.4. This result recalls the evidence produced in Downward (2007), which highlights a strong interdependence between sport participation and education. Therefore, it seems that the degree of literacy reinforces the beneficial impact of sport participation. This might be an important point for policy formulation. But there is no significant association between crime rate and the interaction between sport participation and GDP per capita (sport × GDP per capita).

To summarize the findings about the relationship between crime and sport participation, it is possible to conclude that:

1. there is a robust negative association between sport participation and property crime;
2. there is a robust negative association between sport participation and juvenile crime;
3. there is a positive association between sport participation and violent crime. However, it is only weakly significant at 10 per cent.

As noted above, interestingly, the interaction term between sport participation and literacy (sport × literacy) is negatively associated with crime rates. The association is robust in the case of property crime and juvenile crime. As noted above, this result is akin to that presented in Downward (2007), which highlights a strong inter-dependence between sport participation and education. Therefore, it seems that literacy reinforces the relational beneficial impact of sport participation. In other words, a complementarity between sport and education does exist. In particular, it seems that investments in human capital and sport participation reinforce each other. This recalls the theoretical line expounded recently by the Nobel graduate J.J. Heckman and his associates (see in particular, Heckman, Stixrud and Urzua, 2006; Borghans *et al.*, 2008; Cunha and Heckman, 2009; Heckman, 2009). Their approach draws heavily on psychological studies. In short, individuals have cognitive and non-cognitive abilities. Cognitive abilities are related to education. They take shape and develop especially in early childhood and adolescence. On the other hand, non-cognitive abilities continue to develop even in later years of life. Non-cognitive abilities include perseverance, motivation, self-esteem, self-control, conscientiousness and forward-looking behaviour. As pointed out by Heckman (2009), participation in crime turns out to be relatively more strongly determined by non-cognitive traits or – alternatively – they are associated with pro-social behaviours. What is important to note here is that cognitive and non-cognitive abilities exhibit synergy and complementarity. Briefly, they mutually reinforce each other, so the interaction between sport participation and education can be explained along these lines. In particular, sport participation may be an incubator for non-cognitive abilities which reinforce cognitive abilities provided by educational attainment. Therefore, the higher the educational attainment, the greater will be the benefit of sport participation.

Such a complementarity might work the other way round. Pfeifer and Cornelissen (2010), using waves 2000–2005 of the German Socio-Economic Panel (GSOEP), show that in Germany, sport participation turned out to be beneficial for the educational attainment of individuals. A similar result for the US has been found by Barron, Ewing and Waddell (2000), who show how males involved in high school athletics achieve a level of education higher than the rest of the sample analysed.

CONCLUDING REMARKS

The results of this work shed new light on the relationship between crime and sport participation. A panel dataset was constructed for the 20 Italian regions over the period 1997–2003. Results show that: (i) there is a robust negative association between sport participation and property crime; (ii) there is a robust negative association between sport participation and juvenile crime; and (iii) there is a positive association between sport participation and violent crime, but it is only weakly significant. Therefore, the idea that sport participation can have a role in reducing or preventing crime seems to be confirmed by results (i) and (ii). Interestingly, the interaction term between sport participation and literacy (sport × literacy) is negatively associated with crime rates. Such association is robust in the case of property crime and juvenile crime. In sum, the results are somewhat confused. The channels through which sport participation can affect societal well-being have been interpreted in the light of Kenneth Boulding's theory of social interactions. However, needless to say, stating that sport participation is not detrimental for society is not equivalent to saying that sport participation is surely beneficial for society. Therefore, to study the impact of sport participation on societal and individual well-being, the analysis must necessarily be further deepened.

ACKNOWLEDGEMENTS

Preliminary versions of this work have been presented at: Arbeitskreis Sportökonomik, Sport and Urban Economics, Berlin, 8–9 May 2009; First European Conference in Sports Economics, Paris, 14–15 September 2009, University of Paris-Sorbonne; Conference on Happiness and Relational Goods, Venice, 11–13 June 2009. Financial support from IReR is gratefully acknowledged.

NOTES

1. COM(2007) 391 final, Presented by the Commission: SEC(2007) 932, SEC(2007) 934, SEC(2007) 935, SEC(2007) 936, available at http://ec.europa.eu/sport/white-paper/index_en.htm (April 2009).

2. Boulding writes: 'I recognize three major organizers in society. An organizer is something like a social gene. It is a relationship which organizes role structure in society and hence is capable of developing organization. I distinguish three of these organizers. I call them the threat system, the exchange system and the integrative system' (Boulding, 1968, p. 43). On Boulding's theory of social interactions, see also Caruso (2009b).
3. On the economic interpretation of human sociality see Bardsley and Sugden (2006) and Sacco, Vanin and Zamagni (2006).

REFERENCES

Andreff, W. (2008), Globalization of the Sports Economy, *Rivista di Diritto ed Economia dello Sport*, 4 (3), 13–32.

Bardsley, N. and Sugden, R. (2006), Human Nature and Sociality Economics, in Kolm, S.C. and Ythier, J.M. (eds), *Handbook of the Economics of Giving, Altruism and Reciprocity*, Vol. 1, North-Holland, Elsevier, Amsterdam.

Barron, J.M., Ewing, B.T. and Waddell, G.R. (2000), The Effects of High School Athletic Participation on Education and Labor Market Outcomes, *The Review of Economics and Statistics*, 82 (3), 409–421.

Becchetti, L., Londono Bedoya, D.A. and Trovato, G. (2006), *Income, Relational Goods and Happiness*, Quaderni CEIS No. 227, Tor Vergata University, Rome.

Becchetti, L., Pelloni, A. and Rossetti, F. (2008), Relational Goods, Sociability and Happiness, *Kyklos*, 61 (3), 343–363.

Borghans, L., Duckworth, A.L., Heckman, J.J. and Ter Weel, B. (2008), The Economics and Psychology of Personality Traits, *Journal of Human Resources*, 43 (4), 972–1059.

Boulding, K.E. (1963), Towards a Pure Theory of Threat Systems, *American Economic Review Papers and Proceedings*, 53 (2), 424–434.

Boulding, K.E. (1968), *Beyond Economics: Essays in Society, Religion, and Ethics*, The University of Michigan Press, Ann Arbor, MI.

Boulding, K.E. (1973), *The Economy of Love and Fear*, Wadsworth Publishing Company, Belmont, CA.

Boulding, K.E. (1978), *Ecodynamics: A New Theory of Societal Evolution*, Sage Publications, London.

Britt, C.L. (1997), Reconsidering the Unemployment and Crime Relationship: Variation by Age Group and Historical Period, *Journal of Quantitative Criminology*, 13 (4), 405–428.

Bruni, L. (2006), *Reciprocità, Dinamiche di Cooperazione, Economia e Società Civile*, Bruno Mondatori, Pavia.

Bruni, L. and Stanca, L. (2006), Watching Alone: Relational Goods, Television and Happiness, *Journal of Economic Behavior and Organization*, 65 (3–4), 506–528.

Budzinski, O. and Satzer, J. (2008), *Sports Business and the Theory of Multisided Markets*, Joint Discussion Paper in Economics, Phillips Marburg University, Marburg.

Burdett, K., Lagos, R. and Wright, R. (2003), Crime, Inequality and Unemployment, *The American Economic Review*, 93 (5), 1764–1777.

Campiglio, L. (1990), L'illecito, in IReR, *Tensioni e Nuovi Bisogni della Città in Trasformazione*, Franco Angeli, Milan.

Carter, J.M. (1985), Sport, War and the Three Orders of Feudal Society: 700–1300, *Military Affairs*, 49 (3), 132–139.

Caruso, R. (2009a), Spesa Pubblica e Criminalità Organizzata in Italia: Evidenza Empirica su Dati Panel nel Periodo 1997–2003, *Economia e Lavoro*, 43 (1), 71–88.

Caruso, R. (2009b), Il Pensiero di Kenneth Boulding, Economista Irenico, Relazioni Umane tra Scambio, Dono e Coercizione, *Storia del Pensiero Economico*, 6 (2), 5–30.

Cooper, J. (1989), The Military and Higher Education in the USSR, *Annals of the American Academy of Political and Social Science*, 502, 108–119.

Cornell, T.J. and Allen, T.B. (eds) (2002), *War and Games*, The Boydell Press, Rochester, UK.

Cunha, F. and Heckman, J.J. (2009), The Economics and Psychology of Inequality and Human Development, *Journal of the European Economic Association*, 7 (2–3), 320–364.

Downward, P. (2007), Exploring the Economic Choice to Participate in Sport: Results from the 2002 General Household Survey, *International Review of Applied Economics*, 21 (5), 633–653.

Endresen, I.M. and Olweus, D. (2005), Participation in Power Sports and Antisocial Involvement in Preadolescent and Adolescent Boys, *Journal of Child Psychology and Psychiatry*, 46 (5), 468–478.

Ewing, B.T. (1998a), Athletes and Work, *Economic Letters*, 59, 113–117.

Ewing, B.T. (1998b), High School Athletes and Marijuana Use, *Journal of Drug Education*, 28 (2), 147–157.

Ewing, B.T. (2007), The Labor Market Effect of High School Athletic Participation, *Journal of Sport Economics*, 8 (3), 255–265.

Fort, R. and Quirk, J. (1995), Cross-Subsidization, Incentives and Outcomes in Professional Team Sports Leagues, *Journal of Economic Literature*, 33 (3), 1265–1299.

Forrest, D. and McHale, I. (2009), Public Policy, Sport and Happiness: An Empirical Study, paper presented at the *Annual Conference of Arbeitskreis Sportökonomik*, Sport and Urban Economics, Berlin, 2009.

Gui, B. (2000), Beyond Transactions: On the Interpersonal Dimension of Economic Reality, *Annals of Public and Cooperative Economics*, 71 (1), 139–169.

Hahn, F.H. (1971), Equilibrium with Transaction Costs, *Econometrica*, 39 (3), 417–439.

Heckman, J.J. (2009), Investing in our Young People: Lessons from Economics and Psychology, *Rivista Internazionale di Scienze Sociali*, 117 (3), 22–31.

Heckman, J.J., Stixrud, J. and Urzua, S. (2006), The Effects of Cognitive and Noncognitive Abilities on Labor Market Outcomes and Social Behavior, *Journal of Labor Economics*, 24 (2), 411–482.

Henderson, D.J., Olbrecht, A. and Polachek, S.W. (2006), Do Former College Athletes Earn More at Work? A Nonparametric Assessment, *The Journal of Human Resources*, 41 (3), 558–577.

Howell, R. (1975), The USSR, Sport and Politics Intertwined, *Comparative Education*, 11 (2), 137–145.

Lechner, M. (2009), Long-Run Labour Market and Health Effects of Individual Sports Activities, *Journal of Health Economics*, 28 (4), 839–854.

Levitt, S.D. (2001), Alternative Strategies for Identifying the Link between Unemployment and Crime, *Journal of Quantitative Criminology*, 17 (4), 377–390.

Long, J.E. and Caudill, S.B. (1991), The Impact of Participation in Intercollegiate Atheletics on Income and Graduation, *The Review of Economics and Statistics*, 73 (3), 525–531.

Neale, W. (1964), The Peculiar Economics of Professional Sports: A Contribution to the Theory of the Firm in Sporting Competition and in Market Competition, *Quarterly Journal of Economics*, 78 (1), 1–14.

Overman, S.J. and Terry, T. (1991), Alcohol Use and Attitudes: A Comparison of College Athletes and Nonathletes, *Journal of Drug Education*, 21 (2), 107–117.

Pfeifer, C. and Cornelissen, T. (2010), The Impact of Participation in Sports on Educational Attainment: New Evidence from Germany, *Economics of Education Review*, 29 (1), 94–103.

Riordan, J. (1974), Soviet Sport and Soviet Foreign Policy, *Soviet Studies*, 26 (3), 322–343.

Riordan, J. (1993), The Rise and Fall of Soviet Olympic Champions, *Olympika: The International Journal of Olympic Studies*, 2, 25–44.

Rottenberg, S. (1956), The Baseball Players' Labour Market, *Journal of Political Economy*, 64 (3), 242–258.

Rutten, E.A., Stams, J.M.G.J., Biesta, G.J.J., Schuengel, C., Dirks, E. and Hoeksma, J.B. (2007), The Contribution of Organized Youth Sport to Antisocial and Prosocial Behavior in Adolescent Athletes, *Journal of Youth Adolescence*, 36, 255–264.

Sacco, P., Vanin, P. and Zamagni, S. (2006), The Economics in Human Relationships, in Kolm, S.C. and Ythier, J.M. (eds), *Handbook of the Economics of Giving, Altruism and Reciprocity*, pp. 695–727, North-Holland, Elsevier, Amsterdam.

Scorcu, A.E. and Cellini, R. (1998), Economic Activity in the Long Run: An Empirical Investigation on Aggregate Data from Italy, 1951–1994, *International Review of Law and Economics*, 18 (2), 279–292.

Szymanski, S. (2003), The Economic Design of Sporting Contests, *Journal of Economic Literature*, 41, 1137–1187.

Ulhaner, C.J. (1989), Relational Goods and Participation: Incorporating Sociability into a Theory of Rational Action, *Public Choice*, 62, 253–285.

Zimbalist, A. (2003), Sport as Business, *Oxford Review of Economic Policy*, 19 (4), 503–511.

PART II
The economics of professional team sports

4. Sport financing and governance in Europe

Stefan Szymanski

The Union shall contribute to the promotion of European sporting issues, while taking account of the specific nature of sport, its structures based on voluntary activity and its social and educational function. . .

Union action shall be aimed at . . . developing the European dimension in sport, by promoting fairness and openness in sporting competitions and cooperation between bodies responsible for sports, and by protecting the physical and moral integrity of sportsmen and sportswomen, especially the youngest sportsmen and sportswomen. . .

The Union and the Member States shall foster cooperation with third countries and the competent international organisations in the field of education and sport, in particular the Council of Europe. . .

In order to contribute to the achievement of the objectives referred to in this Article the European Parliament and the Council, acting in accordance with the ordinary legislative procedure, after consulting the Economic and Social Committee and the Committee of the Regions, shall adopt incentive measures, excluding any harmonisation of the laws and regulations of the Member States.

Article 165 of the Lisbon Treaty

INTRODUCTION

With these words, the European Union has acquired what it describes as 'soft' competence in the field of sport. The policy approach of the EU was set out in detail in a White Paper published in 2007 (COM(2007) 391), and in welcoming the new treaty, Michal Krejza, head of the Commission's sports unit, suggested that an EU sports programme could be designed to:

- contribute to the promotion of European values (physical and moral integrity of sportspersons, fairness of competitions):

projects could address issues such as doping, racism and protection of minors;

- foster the social and educational function of sport: projects could address issues such as gender equality, disability and co-operation between sports organisations;
- promote the transfer of knowledge, innovation, dialogue and good governance in the sector: projects could address issues such as licensing rules for clubs and mobility of sports experts;
- contribute to the promotion of a physically active lifestyle: projects could address issues such as health promotion; and
- foster co-operation with third countries and with international organisations in the field of sport.

This chapter discusses some of the challenges that the EU, and European sports organisations more generally, will face in seeking to develop a coherent policy based on these principles. The fundamental problem identified in this chapter is that whereas the treaty recognises the voluntary nature of much sporting activity, the reality of most European sport that is not organised on commercial lines is that it relies on state funding. Implicit in this framework, and explicit in the Commission's previous analysis of sport, is that there exists such a thing as 'the European Model of Sport' and that this model is constructed on the basis of a pyramid where governing bodies manage the sport from above while clubs below simply take part in sporting competitions. In reality, much of the funding for sport within Europe comes from the state, which demands a greater or lesser say in the way funds are disbursed depending on the member state, while a small number of clubs and elite players, who play in highly lucrative leagues and championships, generate large incomes and demand a significant say over the way that their sport is run.

The chapter begins by discussing the contested meanings of sport. There follows an outline of some of the current problems facing sports in Europe, both in terms of finance and governance. It then discusses the weaknesses of the European model and suggests an alternative framework. Finally the chapter considers some future directions that policy might take.

THE CONTESTED MEANINGS OF SPORT

The word 'sport' has many meanings, and these meanings are often applied differently in different countries.[1] The ancient Olympic sports were not originally called 'sports' and originated from religious festivals, while the Roman games were directed at providing a form of mass entertainment (the famous 'bread and circuses'). In medieval times the idea of sport became associated with the pursuits of the leisured nobility – jousting, hunting and the like. In early modern Britain and in the USA, many of the familiar modern sports – football, rugby, cricket, baseball, basketball and hockey – emerged as pastimes for an increasingly leisured middle class. This contrasted with the emergence of gymnastic movements in 19th century Europe, such as the Turnen movement in Germany, which developed on nationalistic and militaristic lines.[2] One important distinction which remains with us today is the issue of competition – while many of the theorists of modern gymnastics and physical education worked in the school system and promoted non-competitive exercise aimed at creating healthy bodies and social solidarity, the sports movement embraced competition to the full, promoting championships and other forms of contest to distinguish winners from losers.[3]

During the Victorian era, the practice of sports was often endowed with a moral dimension, suggesting that it remained in some sense 'noble'; however, the widespread popularity of some sports, especially football, led to their commercial exploitation.[4] From the end of the 19th century, talented players became employees performing for a salary, employed by a commercial organisation concerned with generating an income from paying fans. During the twentieth century, European nationalism turned sports stars into symbols of national pride and turned some sport into a form of 'war without the shooting', as George Orwell put it. In more recent years, the development of a wider interest in fitness has led to phenomena such as jogging, which while not typically defined as a sport, would presumably be thought of as an activity for the *sportif*, and fitness clubs, which typically are not involved in competitive sport but would still consider themselves implicated in Article 165.

It becomes clear that we can mean quite different things when we talk about sport. We may be talking about a form of mass entertainment watched by millions across the globe, we may be talking about the playing out of national rivalries, we may be talking about the dedication of athletes to the achievement of new records in the almost complete absence of an audience, we may be talking about a form of sociability practised in a local community, an aspect of the school curriculum or even a personal quest at the fitness centre played out in private. It may be competitive or non-competitive; it may be highly lucrative or extremely costly; it may be local, regional, national or international. It may be carried out under the auspices of a governing body, or of the state (in schools, for example), or it may be carried out on a completely ad hoc basis by private individuals acknowledging the authority of no one.

CRISES IN FINANCE, CRISES IN GOVERNANCE

European sport is in a state of financial crisis, but there are two very different crises, not one. One crisis concerns the operation of professional sport, principally football, at the highest level. The other crisis exists at the level of grassroots participation, in particular, established local sports clubs.

The Financial Crisis in Professional Sport

Professional football dominates European sport in terms of the level of interest of fans, whether it be attending games, watching on TV or reading newspapers. It is a form of mass entertainment, not dissimilar to movies or soap opera. The teams that succeed are the ones that can attract the greatest level of support, in the same way that other forms of entertainment compete for attention. To achieve this support requires an investment in facilities, skilled labour (players) and marketing, much like any other consumer-oriented business. Many people prefer to think of these football clubs in a different way. They like to think of the club as a representative of a community, sometimes even a statement of political independence. They wish that football was conducted on a high moral plane, where money and commercial operations are not important. They even suggest that this was how football once used to be. Not unnaturally, the clubs themselves like to promote this image, since it helps to attract more fans. However, the fundamentals of the 'football business' have changed little over the last century. In all cases, teams seek to attract the best players by offering the highest wages, which then enables them to attract large crowds whose payments then pay the wages.[5] The extent to which club owners or presidents are able to profit personally from the football business differs significantly both in time and place, but again, making money has always been part of the game.

Financial success is an integral part of sporting success in the European football business. Teams that are unable to fund the acquisition of top quality players will find themselves relegated to a lower level of competition. While many fans are loyal to their team, there is a close positive correlation between the level of success of a club and its annual revenues – a lower level of competition means lower income. Absent the promotion and relegation system, this would no longer be true, since even weak teams could rely on the attractiveness of visiting strong teams to generate income. In the American system of 'closed' leagues, where a league contains a fixed number of franchises and there is no relegation, teams do not have to compete desperately for success, and are indeed willing to agree arrangements among themselves to share revenues and limit spending on players through salary caps.[6] Strong clubs in European leagues will never willingly share substantial parts of their income with weaker clubs so long as the institution of promotion and relegation continues to exist, since it would be tantamount to committing themselves to playing at a lower level of competition, if not in the short term, then eventually.

The European Commission's paper on the European model of sport published in 1998 pointed to concerns expressed by grassroots sports organisations that the 'solidarity' mechanism, by which the national federations are supposed to generate income from high-level sport and pass it down to the grassroots, was not working. But the same document argued that the 'system of promotion and relegation is one of the key features of the European model of sport'.

Given the sporting and financial competition for success, it is not surprising that teams often overstep the mark. Clubs are often guilty of underhand dealings in seeking to attract players, inducing them to breach their contracts with an existing club contrary to FIFA regulations. Clubs overspend in the pursuit of success, putting themselves into financial jeopardy and often requiring financial restructuring. Insolvency is commonplace. In England, where most professional football clubs are limited liability companies required to file annual accounts open to public inspection, around 50 clubs have entered into administration (a process intended to reconcile creditors while relaunching the business as a going concern) over the last 20 years (see Beech *et al.*, 2008). In other countries where club accounts are not open and ownership structures are often less clear, there have been many cases where ownership has changed hands following a financial crisis. In some cases, a wholesale restructuring of clubs has been required as, for example, in Spain in 1991 and France in 1984 (see Ascari and Gagnepain, 2006 and Gouguet and Primault, 2006). The organisation of clubs as a special kind of limited company eschewing the pursuit of profit, or as membership clubs controlled by fans who pay membership fees, has not avoided the problems described here, as is shown by the case of Spain, where clubs using both ownership forms have incurred apparently unmanageable debts (Barajas and Rodriguez, 2010). In more recent years some leagues have attempted to impose tighter financial regulation. In France since 1990, an organisation called the *Direction Nationale de Contrôle de Gestion* (DNCG), established by the national federation, has had the right to oversee the finances of French clubs with a view to preventing them from overextending themselves; in Germany the *Deutsche Fussball Liga* (DFL) has had oversight of club budgets in a way similar to the DNCG. Observers are divided over the effectiveness of these regulations; some (for example, Frick and Prinz, 2006; Gouguet and Primault, 2006) argue that the system is broadly successful while other (for example, Andreff, 2007; Dietl and Franck, 2007) are more sceptical.

The Financial Crisis in Grassroots Sport

The scale of grassroots sports is vast. Across the European Union, around 18 per cent of the population participate in sport at least three times a week, 38 per cent participate at least once a week, and 46 per cent participate at least once a month. Given an EU population of around 500 million, this implies that 190 million EU citizens participate in sport at least once a week, or 230 million participate at least once a month. Given that professional football in Europe is estimated to generate revenues of €14.6 billion per year, and that this probably accounts for at least half of all professional sports revenues in Europe, then even a 50 per cent tax rate on professional sport allocated to the grassroots would amount to little more than €60 per person, about enough to buy a decent pair of running shoes. If we think of sports as a pyramid, with professional teams at the top and mass participation as the base, then the base is very broad indeed.

In reality, sports clubs do not rely heavily on redistribution from above. Andreff (2009) reports survey evidence showing that on average 50 per cent of funding for sports participation in the EU comes from household expenditures, 14 per cent from enterprises and 36 per cent from government (of which two-thirds comes from local government). Practice varies widely across Europe; at one extreme, countries such as Bulgaria and the Czech Republic from the old Soviet bloc still fund sports participation largely through public subsidies, while in the UK, the government contribution to sport is (and always has been) low.

Even before the recession took hold, Breuer and Wicker (2008) reported that one-third of German sports clubs were currently in deficit. Grassroots sports clubs have struggled to make ends meet. On the one hand public subsidies are often harder to obtain because of national budget deficit problems. On the other hand club membership and volunteerism, the mainstay of most grassroots sports, is under pressure. Adults in work find themselves under time pressure, while concerns about child safety have increased regulations, and in many cases adults view leadership of youth sports as being increasingly stressful.

Crisis in Governance

In the world of commercial sport, clubs want a bigger say in the running of national federations, to reflect the significance of their financial contribution. Thirty years ago even the most popular professional sports generated little income; today the development of broadcast technologies and greater awareness of commercial opportunities (for example merchandising and sponsorship) have made the financial scale of professional sport significant. Professional sports have also attracted a number of wealthy and powerful owners (perhaps most notably Silvio Berlusconi in Italy, but in recent years the influx of foreign owners in English Premier League football has drawn most attention). This has raised concerns that the future of professional sport may be controlled by a small number of oligarchs, perhaps with little reverence for national traditions in sport.

The growth in the income gap between the professional levels and the grassroots has also raised controversy. The perception that the big clubs simply use grassroots organisations to groom talent and give nothing back is widespread. At the same time some countries have seen increasing levels of government interference. Sport has always played a role in government policy, but the recognition that an active lifestyle is a key element in controlling weight gain has given an added impetus to public policy. The constant demand for the success of national teams in events such as the Olympics or the FIFA World Cup has ensured a constant level of political oversight. The growth of internet gambling has also threatened the state monopoly of a national lottery, one of the principal sources for funding grassroots sports in many European nations.

THE EUROPEAN MODEL OF SPORT AND THE ELEPHANT IN THE ROOM

The pyramid model, pictured in the 1998 European Commission paper and often referred to since, places European sports federations at the top, national sports federations beneath them, then regional sports federations and grassroots federations and clubs at the base of the pyramid. This model describes a hierarchy (without explaining where the decision-making powers reside) where the base-level clubs represent a form of voluntary activity. This is then contrasted with the American model, which, it is claimed, is more tied to business.

The pyramid model is at best a very sketchy description of the organisation of sport in Europe. One major problem is that the American model, which is claimed to be so different, is not clearly understood or articulated. True, at the professional level, sports are organised as businesses, a statement which is also true of many sports organisations in Europe (for example, football clubs in England have been organised as limited liability companies since the 19th century). But the model neglects entirely the organisation of amateur sport in America, which relies extensively on volunteerism as in Europe, is profoundly integrated into the school and higher education system (much more so than in Europe) and relies extensively on public funding (notably through the parks and recreation departments of municipal and state governments). Thus the identification of the American system with business tells only a small part of the entire story.

Likewise, the description of the European model based on the relationship between private sports federations and their members presents only a part of the picture. In fact, as in America, we can identify three main types of organisation involved in the management of sport:

1. The sports federations: the organisations are primarily devoted to the promotion of amateur sport within the hundreds of thousands of private sports clubs that exist in Europe; most of these clubs are quite small, and organise sport primarily for adults.
2. Private companies: a growing number of providers of sports facilities are private corporations such as fitness clubs, again primarily aimed at adults, often for people with limited time to take on the organisational tasks which preoccupy amateur clubs within the federations. Businesses are involved in many other aspects of sport, from sponsorship and subsidisation of company sports facilities to the production and sale of sporting goods.
3. State and local government: compared to America, the state plays a much larger role in the organisation of sport in Europe. The state plays a key role in the funding of sport in schools, allocating budgets for PE and sports instructors, funding capital and equipment investments and mandating time allocated to sport and PE. The state also plays a large role in funding amateur sports through subsidies (especially through hypothecation of revenues from the state monopoly of lotteries), planning sports investments, promoting sports participation, funding elite sports and underwriting the hosting of major sports events.

From this it should be apparent that the state is 'the elephant in the room' that is seemingly ignored in the pyramid model. True, the 1998 document refers to the fact that the state plays a significant role in the organisation of sports federations in southern European nations, but this scarcely does justice to the key role played in the rest of Europe by the state and by state funding.

The fact that the state is a key player in the European model of sport does not mean that the state controls sports. The communist and fascist models of sport, in which sporting organisations are subordinated to the interests of the state, are widely discredited. European states claim that sports federations are entirely autonomous, and that the role of the state is merely supportive. However, it is not possible to imagine that the state can provide in the region of one-third of the funding for sport in Europe without the budget holders seeking to have some influence over the way sport is organised. There are many obvious examples:

- In many countries, the state sets explicit targets which must be met in order to secure continued funding.
- The decision to bid for hosting a major event such as the Olympics or the FIFA World Cup cannot be undertaken without the explicit support of the government, which also funds some if not all of the capital costs associated with hosting. In return, government expects to gain prestige and to influence the legacy outcomes.
- The state defines the role of sport in school curricula and approves training programmes for teachers of school sport.

If the state does not play a significant role in the organisation of European sports, why do governments have sports ministers, ministries, policies and publications?

Recognition of the fundamental role played by governments in the organisation of European sport is an essential step in defining a European sports model that can help focus on policy dilemmas such as those identified in the previous two sections. The relationship between governments and federations lies at the heart of many of the problems. On the one hand, federations tend to see government as a source of finance, but resist the attempts of government to impose their priorities (as for example, when federations contest legislation concerning free movement of labour, culminating in the Bosman case[7]). On the other hand, governments tend to engage with federations as if they are fully representative of all sport, while assuming that the governance of each federation is a settled matter rather than a contested issue. This neglects the role of both business and 'autonomous', ad hoc sport (where the participants are self-regulated and do not recognise any higher authority), and ignores the fact that many members of sports federations do not consider its leadership to be either democratic or transparent in business and financial dealings.

AN ALTERNATIVE VIEW OF THE EUROPEAN MODEL

This chapter has argued that the well-known pyramid model of European sport neglects or underplays the contributions of the state, private enterprise and ad hoc sports activities to the European sports scene. This neglect distorts the analysis of policy and can lead to distorted conclusions. In particular, a broader framework is required to identify some of the issues facing European sports.

Figure 4.1 presents a matrix description of the key actors in European sports. The rows define the roles of:

purchasers – those who ultimately consume sports-related services,
providers – those who deliver sports-related services,
intermediaries – those who take responsibility for the organisation of relations between purchaser and provider, and regulate the funding of services provided and the price paid by purchasers.

The columns of the matrix define three different decision making systems:

political – where elected representatives make organisational choices on behalf of voters,
associational – where federations co-ordinate voluntary organisations answerable to their members,
commercial – where customers buy services on the market delivered by private enterprise.

The matrix indicates the principal relationships that currently exist within European sport, but it is by no means exhaustive. Thus the first column suggests that the principal role of government is mediating the provision of sport (and PE) in schools to meet the interests of voters. However, in some countries, governments strongly support the provision of sport to children through membership clubs affiliated to governing bodies (for example, in Germany and the Netherlands). In some cases, governments seek to co-ordinate with sports governing bodies to encourage links between schools and member clubs to deliver sports opportunities for children.

The second column covers essentially the activities described in the pyramid model, but instead of placing international federations at

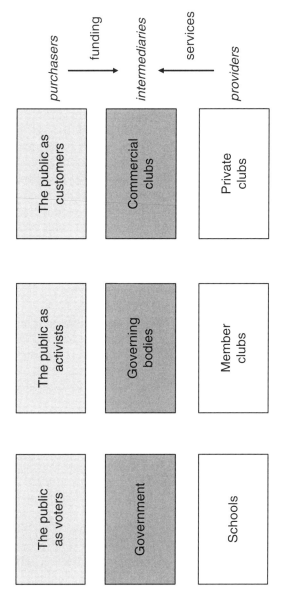

Figure 4.1   The European sports matrix

the top, they are represented simply as intermediaries between clubs and activists. Thus federations do not really control their sport, and if they fail to respond to the concerns of the public, they find their sources of funding drying up. In some cases, federations recognise this reality and thrive, in other cases they become too remote from the clubs they represent and fail to engage with their public.

The third column represents commercial sport. Commercial sports clubs generate income from paying fans and spectators, while recruiting talent from all of the providers. In the pyramid model, the commercial clubs are controlled by the federations, but in reality the commercial clubs have become more and more powerful in running the federations, since they have significant economic interests to defend. Private clubs that deliver sports services to paying customers also play an important role (although their role in supplying commercial clubs with talent is at present limited); this is largely ignored in the existing policy debates.

The organisation of the matrix does not imply any necessary relationship between actors on the sports scene, either in theory or in practice. Rather, it highlights the range of possibilities that exist, and the underlying complexity of the relationship between citizens, club federations, government and private enterprise.

CONCLUSIONS

The European sports model is in crisis. While there is widespread alarm about the state of commercially organised sport, this chapter argues that the real crisis lies in the provision of grassroots, participatory sports.

Understanding the current crisis is made more difficult by the limitations of the well-known pyramid model, which mistakenly characterises European sport as the exclusive domain of sports federations, whereas in reality the state and private enterprise play a significant role. This chapter presents a matrix model as a more realistic and more informative way of explaining the key relationships in European sport.

Two specific conclusions can be drawn from the foregoing analysis. First, voluntary participatory sport is coming under increasing funding pressure because of the withdrawal of government support, itself a consequence of the crisis in European public finances. Similar

problems are likely to emerge, if they have not already, in the provision of sport in schools. Yet public policy, especially in the face of
the growing obesity crisis, is placing more emphasis on the importance of an active lifestyle than ever before. If public funding is not
forthcoming, it may be that partnership between the private and
public sectors will become far more important in the future, raising
issues as to how sports federations will respond to these challenges
and opportunities.

Second, the location of commercial sport under the control of
sports federations primarily responsible to grassroots sports is
increasingly problematic. There are fundamental inconsistencies
between the objectives of commercial and participatory sport, and
their integration within a single governance structure risks satisfying
no one. One option that merits consideration is the formal separa-
tion of commercial sport from amateur sport, while accepting the
possibility of mobility from one organisational structure to another.
It is a simple accounting mistake to believe that commercial sport
has the capacity to fund grassroots sports to any significant extent.
In the end, the funding of participatory sport will come primarily
from member fees and subscriptions or the taxpayer.

NOTES

1. See for example Guttmann (2004) for a thorough account of the development of
    sports.
2. See for example Ueberhorst (1978) or Guttmann (1994).
3. A good discussion of the historical evolution of physical education can be found
    in Van Dalen *et al.* (1953).
4. Tranter (1998) provides a very useful discussion of the transition that took place
    in the Victorian era.
5. This was true even in Stalinist Russia – see Edelman (1993), pp. 67–8.
6. See Hoehn and Szymanski (1999) for a comparison of the European and
    American models.
7. In 1990, Jean-Marc Bosman, a 25-year-old veteran player, reached the end of his
    contract with the Belgian club Royal Football Club de Liège, and started negoti-
    ating his transfer to a French club in Dunkirk. He rejected the Belgian club's offer
    to play the next season for the minimum wage, that is, two-thirds of his current
    remuneration. RFC Liège opposed his transfer to Dunkirk, leaving Bosman the
    choice of continuing in Liège or giving up his career as a professional player; he
    considered this unfair and took the club to court. Although the court delivered a
    judgement that he was free to move to another club, Bosman was boycotted by
    both the Belgian and international football federations. In 1995, the European
    Court of Justice finally abolished the previous restrictive transfer system as well as
    the so-called '3 + 2' rule which allowed any club to field no more than five foreign

players (of which two had trained in the club) in official football games and contests. These restrictions were judged in contradiction to the article of the Treaty of Rome that guarantees any citizen of an EU country free labour mobility in the European unified market.

REFERENCES

Andreff, W. (2007), 'French Football: A Financial Crisis Rooted in Weak Governance', *Journal of Sports Economics*, 8, 652–661.

Andreff, W. (2009) 'Public and Private Sport Financing in Europe: The Impact of Financial Crisis', paper presented at the *84th Western Economic Association International Conference*, Vancouver, 29 June–3 July.

Ascari, G. and Gagnepain, P. (2006), 'Spanish Football', *Journal of Sports Economics*, 7, 76–89.

Barajas, A. and Rodríguez, P. (2010) 'Spanish Football Clubs' Finances: Crisis and Player Salaries', *International Journal of Sport Finance*, 5, 52–66.

Beech, J., Horsman, S. and Magraw, J. (2008), *The Circumstances in which English Football Clubs become Insolvent*, Centre for the International Business of Sport working paper series no.4, Coventry: Coventry University.

Breuer, C. and Wicker, P. (2008), *Public Subsidisation of Sports Clubs*, working paper, Cologne: Deutsche Sporthochschule Köln, Institut für Sportökonomie und Sportmanagement.

Dietl, H.M. and Franck, E. (2007), 'Governance Failure and Financial Crisis in German Football', *Journal of Sports Economics*, 8, 662–669.

Edelman, R. (1993), *Serious Fun: A History of Spectator Sports in the USSR*, Oxford: Oxford University Press.

European Commission (1998), *The European Model of Sport*, Consultation paper of DG X, Brussels.

Frick, B. and Prinz, J. (2006), 'Crisis? What Crisis? Football in Germany', *Journal of Sports Economics*, 7, 60–75.

Gouguet, J.-J. and Primault, D. (2006), 'The French Exception', *Journal of Sports Economics*, 7, 47–59.

Guttmann, A. (1994), *Games and Empires*, New York: Columbia University Press.

Guttmann, A. (2004), *Sports: The First Five Millennia*, Amherst, MI: University of Massachusetts Press.

Hoehn, T. and Szymanski, S. (1999) 'The Americanization of European Football', *Economic Policy*, 28, 205–240.

Tranter, N. (1998), *Sport, Economy and Society in Britain 1750–1914*, Cambridge: Cambridge University Press, 15–16.

Ueberhorst, H. (1978), *Friedrich Ludwig Jahn: 1778/1978*, Bonn: Heinz Moos Verlag.

Van Dalen, D., Mitchell, E. and Bennett, B. (1953), *A World History of Physical Education*, New York: Prentice Hall.

5. The effect on player transfers of a luxury tax on club payrolls: the case of Major League Baseball

Joel G. Maxcy

INTRODUCTION

The 1997 collective bargaining agreement (CBA) between the Major League Baseball (MLB) owners and the players' union introduced a luxury tax on club payrolls. The purpose of the tax was to restrain spending by the highest revenue-producing clubs, for the purpose of enhancing competitive balance. The 2003 CBA extended the luxury tax, which was renamed the competitive balance tax, through the 2006 season, with some modifications. The 2007 CBA extends the tax system virtually unchanged through the 2011 season. Concurrently, also under the pretext of improving competitive balance, the 1997 CBA also introduced an innovative system of sharing local revenue, considerably altering MLB's system for collecting and redistributing club-generated revenues. Under the previous system, the sharing of club-generated income in MLB consisted of primarily a small, fixed percentage, of gate receipts due the visiting club.[1] A cross-subsidization system where all locally produced revenue was taxed and shared replaced a simple gate-sharing method.

Conventional wisdom holds that payroll constraints, in the form of a rigid payroll cap or a less rigid luxury tax on club payrolls, will diminish problems of competitive imbalance in a professional sports league. The economic effects of payroll constraints in professional sports leagues have been examined by a number of writers. Included are Fort and Quirk (1995), who showed that payroll caps improve balance and also depress player salaries. Vrooman (1996) and Rascher (1997) each provided substantiation that under certain circumstances, payroll limitations improve competitive balance.

Table 5.1   Coefficient of variation (payrolls and revenue)

Year	Payroll	Total Revenue	Gate Revenue
1990	0.222	0.304	0.374
1991	0.252	0.289	0.367
1992	0.304	0.281	0.364
1993	0.304	0.256	0.333
1994	0.263	0.292	0.339
1995	0.278	0.387	0.417
1996	0.314	0.300*	0.477
1997	0.339	0.334*	0.525
1998	0.375	0.327*	0.528
1999	0.445	0.329*	0.530
2000	0.393	0.292*	0.525
2001	0.379	0.296*	0.491
2002	0.366	0.291*	0.558
2003	0.396	0.248*	0.578
2004	0.475	0.254*	0.619
2005	0.469	0.210*	0.546
90-2005	0.348	0.293	0.475
90-96	0.277	0.301	0.382
97-05	0.404	0.281	0.544
(t-value difference)	−6.27[a]	−0.694	−7.19[a]

Notes:
*   After redistribution of pooled revenues
a   significant at the 0.01 level

Source: Reprinted from Maxcy (2009), p. 278, with the kind permission of Springer Science and Business Media.

Payroll and revenue data from the 1990 through 2005 seasons, as calculated by Maxcy (2009), are presented in Table 5.1. Reported are calculations of the coefficient of variation on payroll and total revenue (TR) dispersion (TR after redistribution since 1996) and gate revenue dispersion, the best available proxy for local revenue variation.[2] The table shows evidence of increased payroll dispersion throughout the period. There is also evidence that payroll dispersion has increased in the luxury tax period. However, it is not clear if this is because the restraints are not working to alter the incentives of high revenue clubs, or if low revenue clubs are falling farther behind, or else if there has been a change in the goals of the owners.

Two elements of luxury taxes are important: the threshold and the rate. The threshold defines the payroll amount that triggers payment of the tax and the rate is the percentage collected by the league based only on the difference between the club's payroll and the threshold. For example, if the threshold is set at $100m and the tax rate is 50 per cent, a club with a payroll of $150m will pay a tax of $25m.

The 1997 CBA represented a threshold that was allowed to adjust upward in response to club behavior. The tax applied only to the five highest spending teams for each of the 1997–1999 seasons. These teams were taxed on the amount by which their payroll exceeded the threshold, which was defined as the midpoint between the 5th and 6th highest team payrolls. The tax rates were fixed at 35 per cent for 1997–1998 and at 34 per cent for 1999. From the owners' perspective, the flaw in the floating threshold was that the more the high payroll clubs spent on players, the higher the tax threshold, and the restraint on payroll escalation was this negligible.

The 2003 CBA changed the term to *competitive balance tax*; however, a more substantial factor was that the tax had concrete payroll thresholds, which increased each year of the CBA. These were respectively: 2003, $117m; 2004, $120.5m; 2005, $128m; and 2006, $136.5m. The tax rates were 17.5 per cent for 2003 and increased to 22.5 per cent for 2004 and 2005, but these rates applied only to those clubs exceeding the threshold for the first time. Teams over the threshold in consecutive years were taxed at rates of 30 per cent in the second year and 40 per cent in year three.

THEORETICAL MODEL

The model is a modification of that developed by Atkinson *et al.* (1988) that assumes a league of n clubs, each with separate ownership. The league objective is profit maximization by way of maximizing the profits of each club so that

$$\prod = \sum_{i=1}^{n} \pi_i. \tag{5.1}$$

Club profits are simply the difference in total revenues, which includes all retained, locally generated revenue plus all monies redistributed to each club through the league's central fund CF, and total costs (TC) so that

$$\pi_i = TR_i - TC_i. \tag{5.2}$$

Each club's local revenue LR_i is a function of its win percentage w, which is in turn a function of its talent investment t, and local demand characteristics D_i including metropolitan population, per capita income and stadium factors. Thus

$$LR_i(w(t)D_i). \tag{5.3}$$

The profit function for a club in a league employing revenue sharing is modeled as follows:

$$\pi_i = (1 - \alpha)LR_i(w(t)D_i) + \alpha/n\sum_{j=1}^{n}[LR_j(w(t)D_j) + CF]$$
$$- [ct_i + \mu(\rho ct_i)] \tag{5.4}$$

where α is the fraction of revenue each club contributes to the pool. For the sake of simplicity, only the variable cost of talent is included in the cost function. The talent market is assumed to have a finite number of players, and thus represents a zero sum game, as talent hired by one club is denied the others. The variable costs ct_i are determined as the number of units of talent hired at a cost of c per unit. With a luxury tax/competitive balance tax placed on payrolls exceeding a set threshold, the cost function is represented as $TC = ct_i + \mu(\rho ct_i)$, where ρ designates the tax rate, and $\mu = 1$ for clubs exceeding the payroll threshold and 0 otherwise.

The first order condition is

$$(1 - \alpha)\sum_{j=1}^{n}\frac{\partial LR_i}{\partial w_j}\frac{\partial w_j}{\partial t_i} + \frac{\alpha}{n}\sum_{j=1}^{n}\sum_{k=1}^{n}\frac{\partial LR_j}{\partial w_i}\frac{\partial w_k}{\partial t_i} - [c + \mu\rho c] = 0 \quad (5.5)$$

Signing (5.5) reveals a positive first term offset by negative second and third terms. The negative third term indicates that theoretically a luxury tax reduces the incentive to hire talent beyond the tax threshold.

DATA AND EMPIRICAL MODEL

Typically, measures of win dispersion are used to evaluate changes in competitive balance. However, the period of analysis in this study is insufficiently long. Changes in the distribution of talent can be observed in more detail by analyzing player mobility across clubs. An empirical model of player transfers in the context of a luxury tax is developed and tested for both formulations of the tax in MLB, following the method used by Maxcy (2009). The data are derived from the full set (excluding pitchers) of MLB batting statistics for 10 270 player-year observations for all MLB non-pitchers from the 1990 through the 2005 championship seasons.[3] Eliminated from the full sample are observations indicating separations from the club where the player did not transfer, but exited MLB. All within-season transfer observations are removed, so as to include only the between-season labor market. For statistical significance, all player-year observations representing fewer than 30 plate appearances are also excluded. The 2005 player-year observations include the transfers of players based on their club assignment for the 2006 season. Therefore, all between-season trading and signing periods covered through the 2003 CBA are included. The final analysis represents 6981 player-year observations, and includes 1837 transfers by players to other MLB clubs completed during the inter-season trading markets. Summary statistics for the transferring player observations are shown in Table 5.2.

Club-year characteristics that reveal motivation for participation in the between-season labor market are at the heart of this analysis. The inter-season transfer market, composed primarily of trades, free agent signings and the acquisition of players released by other clubs, is motivated by the club's assessment of each player's expected marginal revenue product (MRP). Each player is expected to be retained by, or move to, the club representing his highest-value user. Talent flows (the movement of productive players) are governed by two potentially offsetting forces. First, moves toward higher revenue producers are expected. However, a productive player's expected marginal product is also potentially greater for lower win clubs, setting in motion a natural flow of talent from better to worse performing clubs. Thus poor performing clubs from markets with high revenue potential are likely to be most active in the talent acquisition markets.

Table 5.2 Summary statistics: transfers only

	1990–2005 1837 Observations		1990–1996 696 Observations		1997–2002 732 Observations		2003–2005 409 Observations	
	Mean	SD	Mean	SD	Mean	SD	Mean	SD
AGE	29.899	3.783	29.371	3.604	30.086	3.860	30.462	3.835
FREEAGENT	0.516	0.500	0.522	0.500	0.480	0.500	0.572	0.495
TRADE	0.283	0.450	0.284	0.451	0.281	0.450	0.281	0.450
PRESWITCH	0.689	0.463	0.621	0.486	0.713	0.453	0.763	0.426
OPS	0.697	0.126	0.685	0.124	0.705	0.126	0.705	0.130
GOLDGLOVE	0.039	0.194	0.042	0.200	0.034	0.182	0.044	0.205
CATCHER	0.159	0.366	0.138	0.345	0.165	0.372	0.183	0.387
SHORTSTOP	0.077	0.266	0.070	0.256	0.068	0.252	0.103	0.304
NLtoNL	0.284	0.451	0.246	0.431	0.324	0.468	0.276	0.448
NLtoAL	0.247	0.431	0.250	0.433	0.219	0.414	0.293	0.456
ALtoNL	0.234	0.423	0.227	0.419	0.223	0.416	0.264	0.441
ALtoAL	0.236	0.425	0.277	0.448	0.235	0.424	0.166	0.373
COHESIVE	1.009	0.278	1.006	0.222	1.006	0.273	1.021	0.359
DWIN	−0.004	0.102	−0.003	0.091	−0.001	0.106	−0.010	0.111
DGATE	0.012	0.682	0.005	0.552	0.020	0.724	0.009	0.798
RATIOWP	1.014	0.214	1.011	0.190	1.022	0.221	1.005	0.238
RATIOGATE	1.291	1.062	1.151	0.618	1.400	1.305	1.334	1.148

In order to evaluate whether the luxury tax has altered the flow of talent to the higher revenue clubs, win percentages and normalized gate revenue for the clubs employing the player in the season before the transfer are incorporated along with a variable that indicates a club's tendency actively to engage the talent market.[4] Variables on player characteristics and league modifications that are expected a priori to influence the likelihood of transfer are included for each observation. Individual player attributes include age, performance, defensive position, negotiation status, and whether the player has previously transferred. We restrict the actual analysis to the observations of players actually transferring between teams. Included are the observations of players who transferred as free agents, were traded, or were released by one club and re-signed with a different club. Theoretically, players transfer to a higher-valued user, as defined by differences in the player's expected MRP. Isolation of the effects on the highest revenue-producing clubs needs confirmation to test for the effects of the luxury tax. Given a luxury tax, clubs in the highest revenue quartile have the greatest incentive to reduce their level of talent procurement. A logit model is employed for the purpose of isolating these effects. The tested sample is restricted to the 1837 transfer observations. Binomial dependent variables indicate, with a value of one, whether the player has transferred to a revenue quartile-one club. The coefficient estimates thus compare transfers involving the quartile-one clubs to transfers involving all other teams. To account for the possibility that transfers of the best-performing players are of most consequence in regard to the luxury tax, the model is also tested for players in the top quintile of OPS (On-Base Percentage plus Slugging Average) production for each sample year. The logit model is specified as follows:

$$
\begin{aligned}
REVQ1_{t+1} = {} & \beta_0 + \beta_1 AGE_{it} + \beta_2\, FA + \beta_3 TRADE_{it} \\
& + \beta_4 PRESWITCH_{it} + \beta_5 PROD_{it} \\
& + \beta_6 POSITION_{it} + \beta_7 LEAGUE_t\, toLEAGUE_{t+1} \\
& + \beta_8 TEAMCOHESION + \beta_9 1997BA \\
& + \beta_{10} 2003BA + \beta_{11} DWIN_{tit}\, (RATIOWIN_{it}) \\
& + \beta_{12} DGATE_{tit}\, (RATIOGATE_{it}) + e. \quad (5.6)
\end{aligned}
$$

Explanation of the variables follows:

REVQ1$_{t+1}$: A dummy variable coded 1 for the player's $t + 1$ club when in the first revenue-generating quartile for the observation year t, 0 otherwise. The variable indicates that the player transferred to a quartile-one club.

AGE$_{it}$: A variable measuring player i's age in calendar years as of 30 June of season t.

FA$_{it}$: A binomial variable, coded 1 if the player-year observation indicates free agent status at the completion of year t, 0 otherwise. Players with six or more years of MLB service are granted free agent status at the end of a current contract and may initiate transfers themselves, while others may transfer only at club discretion.

TRADE: A dummy variable coded 1 if the player is transferred directly between clubs by trade for one or more player(s), or a cash sale, 0 otherwise. Included with *FA*, this variable provides an indicator as to the three ways by which players transfer: direct trade or sale between clubs, status as a free agent, or release and re-sign with another club. The latter represents the control group.

PRESWITCH$_{it}$: A binomial dummy variable, coded 1 if the player-year observation indicates a previous transfer for player i, so that the player was not with his original MLB club, 0 otherwise. A player who has never transferred may have greater firm-specific human capital, or clubs may react irrationally to sunk training costs, as they have more player development costs invested in players trained in their minor league systems. Either scenario yields an a priori positive coefficient estimate.

PRODUCTION$_{it}$: A vector of variables that indicate the player's production during the observation year. On-Base-Percentage plus Slugging Average (OPS) is employed to capture batting skill independent of team factors. The Gold Glove award is used to proxy defensive performance. A dummy variable is used to indicate players who are within two years of receiving the award, so that observations for players receiving a Gold Glove award in year t are coded 1 in years t, $t + 1$ and $t + 2$.

POSITION$_{it}$: A vector of dummy variables, coded to represent the more important defensive positions of catcher and shortstop (more than 50 per cent of their game appearances in these positions) in year t.

LEAGUE$_t$ to *LEAGUE*$_{t+1}$: A vector of dummy variables indicating the league affiliation of the clubs surrounding the transfer. The options represented as variables are: transfers between two National League clubs, NL to NL; transfers from a National League club to an American League club, NL to AL; transfers from an American League club to a National League club, AL to NL. Transfers between two American League clubs, AL to AL are excluded from the regressions and represent the control variable. A significant rule difference, potentially affecting talent flows, is that only American League clubs employ a designated hitter. The expectation is that this may increase the flow of older talent, or those otherwise less able to play a fielding position away from NL clubs.

TEAMCOHESION$_j$:   This variable measures the tendency toward stability of club j's roster. The variable is calculated as the percentage of the team's offensive production, measured by plate appearances, represented by players who return to the club for the following season. Each club's average cohesion measure is calculated for each of the three collective bargaining periods represented in the sample, and normalized as a percentage of MLB cohesion for that period.

1997BA: A dummy variable capturing the effects of the 1997 Basic Agreement. The years 1997–2002 are coded 1, and 0 otherwise.

2003BA: A dummy variable capturing the effects of the 2003 Basic Agreement. The years 2003–2005 are coded 1, and 0 otherwise.

DGATE$_{it}$:   The difference in normalized gate revenue (the ratio of each club's total gate revenue to the MLB mean gate revenue for each year t) between the player's before and after transfer clubs in observation year t, constructed as normalized gate revenue of the player's new club minus the normalized gate revenue of the player's original club.

RATIOGATE$_{it}$:   The ratio of normalized gate revenue constructed as normalized gate revenue of the player's new club divided by the normalized gate revenue of the player's original club.

DWIN$_{it}$:   The difference in win percentage between the player's before and after transfer clubs in the observation year t, constructed as the winning percentage of the player's new club minus the winning percentage of the player's original club.

RATIOWIN$_{it}$:   The ratio in win percentage constructed as win percentage of the player's new club divided by the win percentage of the player's original club.

Table 5.3 Revenue quartile models for transfers: differences model

	Full sample: N=1837		1st Quintile: N=220	
	0=1387	1=450	0=147	1=73
	Coefficient	**t-statistic**	**Coefficient**	**t-statistic**
CONSTANT	−4.961[a]	−6.19	−7.277[a]	−1.770
AGE	0.055[a]	2.48	0.093	1.460
FREEAGENT	0.326[c]	1.68	−0.977	−1.080
TRADE	0.028	0.12	−1.909[c]	−1.970
PRESWITCH	0.459[a]	2.59	0.131	0.240
OPS	1.259[b]	2.02	2.842	0.820
GOLDGLOVE	0.790[b]	2.33	1.027	1.210
CATCHER	−0.311	−1.55	−1.690[c]	−1.750
SHORTSTOP	0.144	0.56	−0.392	−0.280
NLtoNL	−0.204	−1.04	−0.227	−0.410
NLtoAL	−0.196	−0.95	0.231	0.390
ALtoNL	−0.482[b]	−2.24	−0.173	−0.240
COHESIVE	0.373	1.44	1.436[b]	1.930
BA97	−0.124	−0.78	0.819	1.540
BA03	−0.220	−1.12	−0.809	−1.290
DWIN	0.494	0.63	−0.526	−0.210
DGATE	2.998[a]	17.62	4.084[a]	6.220
Pseudo R²		0.361		0.471

Notes:
a significant at the 0.01 level; b significant at the 0.05 level; c significant at the 0.1 level.
Dependent variable: $REVQ1_{t1}$ (transfers to revenue quartile 1).

Estimates of the models for transfers to revenue quartile one are shown in Table 5.3. Models that replace $DWIN_{tit}$ with $RATIOWIN_{it}$ and $DGATE_{tit}$ with $RATIOGATE_{it}$ are shown in Table 5.4.

When comparing transfers to quartile-one clubs to the entire set of transfers we see that these players are typically older, and more likely to have transferred clubs previously. As predicted, players transferring to the highest revenue producers are also more productive, in terms of both OPS and Gold Glove awards for defensive play. These players are also significantly less likely to transfer from the AL to the NL, which may indicate that the difference in the designator hitter rule is established for transfer decisions on some players.

Table 5.4   Revenue quartile models for transfers: ratios model

	Full sample: N=1837		1st Quintile: N=220	
	0=1387	1=450	0=147	1=73
	Coefficient	t-statistic	Coefficient	t-statistic
CONSTANT	−6.750[a]	−8.22	−9.533[a]	−2.41
AGE	0.048[b]	2.39	0.070	1.21
FREEAGENT	0.315[c]	1.75	−0.777	−0.99
TRADE	0.011	0.05	−1.632[c]	−1.93
PRESWITCH	0.505[a]	3.06	0.261	0.51
OPS	1.264[b]	2.21	3.260	1.06
GOLDGLOVE	0.803[a]	2.70	0.791	1.01
CATCHER	−0.273	−1.48	−1.488	−1.49
SHORTSTOP	0.247	1.05	−0.386	−0.3
NLtoNL	−0.279	−1.57	−0.001	0
NLtoAL	−0.038	−0.21	0.463	0.85
ALtoNL	−0.617[a]	−3.12	−0.322	−0.48
COHESIVE	0.104	0.43	0.996	1.52
BA97	−0.160	−1.09	0.460	1.00
BA03	−0.241	−1.36	−1.148[c]	−1.81
RATIOWIN	1.190[a]	3.70	0.592	0.54
RATIOGATE	1.212[a]	14.31	2.243[a]	5.82
Pseudo R²		0.237		0.378

Notes:
a significant at the 0.01 level; b significant at the 0.05 level; c significant at the 0.1 level.
Dependent variable: $REVQ1_{t1}$ (transfers to revenue quartile 1).

Most importantly, the results provide general support for the effectiveness of the luxury tax. The results are not statistically significant in most specifications, but are always signed to indicate the effectiveness of the tax, showing that transfers to quartile-one clubs are reduced by the luxury tax. The reformulating of the tax in 2003, with preset thresholds and increased rates for repeat offenders, appears to be effective as well. The effects of the tax are most evident when examining the transfer patterns of the top quintile of players.

Popular wisdom suggests that luxury taxes are not effective in restraining spending by high revenue teams. Critics of the MLB system often maintain that a hard salary cap, such as that employed by the National Football League and National Hockey League are necessary to more equitably distribute talent. While these results cannot determine whether the luxury tax is more or less effective than a salary cap, it does appear that the tax has provided some level of restraint on large market teams.

NOTES

1. The American League (AL) gate split was an 80 per cent:20 per cent home team to visiting team ratio; the National League (NL) home team share was 95 per cent.
2. Data on MLB club finances, including breakdowns by revenue source, are compiled from a variety of sources and collected at Rodney Fort's *Sports Business Data Pages*. Sources include *Financial World* 1990–1996, *Forbes* 1997–2005, MLB Commissioner's Office 2001. The revenue source data are not consistent through the time period in regard to total local revenue by club. It is variously reported only before revenue sharing, only after revenue sharing, or not at all. Total gate revenue produced by each club is reported consistently throughout the period.
3. Pitcher observations are excluded because batting statistics, which are principal to the analysis, are not the chief component of their performance.
4. Gate revenue is chosen as a proxy for local revenue as it is the best revenue source for which data are available throughout the entire sample period, and the local revenue source that is most responsive to variation in win percentage.

REFERENCES

Atkinson, S., Stanley, L. and Tschirhart, J. (1988), 'Revenue Sharing as an Incentive in an Agency Problem: An Example from the National Football League', *Rand Journal of Economics*, **9** (1), 27–43.

Fort, R. (2009), *Sports business pages*, http://www.rodneyfort.com, accessed 15 November 2009.

Fort, R. and Quirk, J. (1995), 'Cross-Subsidization, Incentives, and Outcomes in Professional Team Sports', *Journal of Economic Literature*, **33** (3), 1265–1299.

Major League Baseball (1997), *1997–2000 (2001) Basic Agreement*, http://mlb.mlb.com/pa/pdf/cba_english.pdf, accessed 19 July 2010.

Major League Baseball (2003), *2003–2006 Basic Agreement*, http://bizofbaseball.com/docs/2002_2006basicagreement.pdf, accessed 19 July 2010.

Major League Baseball (2007), *2007–2011 Basic Agreement*, http://mlb.mlb.com/pa/pdf/cba_english.pdf, accessed 13 July 2010.

Maxcy, J.G. (2009) 'Progressive Revenue Sharing in MLB: The Effect on Player Transfers and Talent Distribution', *Review of Industrial Organization*, **35** (3), 275–297.

Rascher, D. (1997), 'A Model of a Professional Sports League', in W. Hendricks (ed.), *Advances in the Economics of Sport*, Greenwich, CT: JAI Press, 27–76.

Vrooman, J. (1996), 'The Baseball Players' Labor Market Reconsidered', *Southern Economic Journal*, **63** (2), 339–360.

6. The role of information in professional football and the German football betting market

Frank Daumann and Markus Breuer

1. INTRODUCTION

The situation for sport betting in Germany is anything but clear from a legal point of view. Since the public provider *Oddset*, run by the German Lotto-Toto-Block, started its business in 2000, several private companies, such as *Bwin* (formerly known as *bet and win*) have also wanted to offer sport betting to German citizens. Local laws accept public monopolies in cases where this constraint reflects public concerns, like the prevention of pathological gambling. In 2006, the German Constitutional Court declared the present monopoly to be illegal (Daumann/Breuer, 2008). Despite that decision, private betting is a grey area in law in Germany. Figures like turnover have to be regarded carefully, as online providers operating from foreign states account for a large part of the market.

From an economic point of view, betting markets provide an ideal arena for testing market efficiency (Brailsford *et al.*, 1995; Gray/ Gray, 1997). In contrast to financial markets, which are normally the focus of efficiency studies, outcomes in sports are well defined (Brailsford *et al.*, 1995). An aspect which has not been analysed so far is the question of the influence of the information level during a season.

In general, we can assume an increasing amount of information concerning the strength of single players and whole teams (in team sports), as well as injuries and so on, from the first match on. That information has to be processed by bookmakers, as well as bettors, and should enhance forecasts regarding the outcome of single matches.

This chapter focuses on the question whether this assumption can be verified in the case of the German major football[1] league (*Bundesliga*): do betting odds, implying the winning probabilities for single matches, become more precise during a season? We concentrate on professional football for the simple reason that this is the most important sport in Germany, bearing the brunt of media attendance and hence, providing the highest level of public information.

The chapter is structured as follows: section two provides an overview of the literature dealing with the context of sport bets; section three explains the correlation between information level and prediction of the outcome of a football match from a theoretical point of view. This model is reappraised in section four on the basis of five football seasons and their betting odds provided by *Oddset*. Sections five and six discuss the findings and offer an outlook.

2.   FORMER STUDIES AND PARTICULARITIES IN THE ANALYSIS OF BETTING MARKETS

Betting markets, especially in the US, have been the subject of several recent studies. To name just a few, Zuber/Gandar/Bowers (1985), Gandar *et al.* (1988), Gray/Gray (1997) and Dare/Holland (2004) analysed the National Football League, while Paul/Weinbach/Weinbach (2003) explored college football. Gandar/Zuber/Dare (2000), Paul/Weinbach/Wilson (2004) and Paul/Weinbach (2005) focused on professional basketball (NBA), Brown/Abraham (2002) and Gandar *et al.* (2002) on baseball (MLB) and finally Woodland/Woodland (2001) and Gandar/Zuber/Johnson (2004) on the National Hockey League (NHL).

Most of these authors concentrated on the question of market efficiency in betting markets. As far as we know, Pankoff (1968) can be regarded as the first dealing with this question from a scientific point of view.[2] In most cases, the efficiency of accessing information on a market is analysed for financial markets. The work of Fama (1970) and his later papers (Fama, 1991, 1998) can be regarded as the foundation for this research field. A market is efficient if (i) there are no transaction costs, (ii) all information is available without cost to all market participants and (iii) all individuals agree on the implications of current information for the current price (Fama, 1970). These assumptions are unrealistic, but they are sufficient for market efficiency and necessary (ibid.). Moreover, Fama differentiates between efficiency in a weak form (all central published information from the past is reflected in prices), a semi-strong form (in addition, all other obviously public information such as information from annual reports is reflected) and finally a strong form (even insider information is considered in the price). The results for betting markets in the US are ambivalent: Gandar *et al.* (1988) were not able to reject the hypothesis that market forecasts in the form of betting lines are unbiased predictors of actual game outcomes. In an older study, Vergin/Scriabin (1978) were able to show that there are exploitable biases in the setting of point spreads in the case of the NFL. Baryla *et al.* (2007) detected a bias in early NBA seasons which can be exploited by bettors.

Findings from studies dealing with US sports (especially American football) and soccer (European football) cannot be directly compared because of a different arrangement of bets: in the case of NFL bets, the bettor has two opportunities: first, he can bet on the victory of any team; second, he can bet on the spread, which means the difference in points between the winning and the losing team. Gray/Gray (1997) underline the problems relating to the second version: standard OLS regressions should not be used as their sensitivity to extreme outliers makes the results difficult to interpret. In the case of European football, bookmakers know only three conclusions of any match: home victory, away victory or draw. These outcomes are denoted as 1, 2, 0 respectively in Germany.[3] Bets on the spread are unknown.[4]

Most studies analysing both the betting market and European soccer, concentrate on the UK. As one of the first, Stefani (1983) investigated the relationship between costs and wagers (not just in England). The higher the cost of a bet, the smaller is the overall amount of money invested; bettors tend to be more selective. Pope/Peel (1989) examined the efficiency of the football betting market in the UK. On the one hand, they noted the absence of trading possibilities that generate abnormal profits (which supports the theory of efficient markets); on the other hand, they pointed out that the odds for the outcome 'draw' do not fully reflect the available information. Dixon/Coles (1997) were able to develop a strategy for English football betting that implies a higher potential than just betting by chance. Cain/Law/Peel (2000) proved a favourite-longshot bias for the Premier League. In contrast, Dixon/Pope (2004) rejected the assumption of an efficient market, because of a reverse (!) favourite-longshot bias. Forrest/Goddard/Simmons (2005) found an answer to the question whether a bettor or a computer program provides more precise forecasts for the outcome of football matches: early in the season, the software shows a better performance; by the end of a season it is exactly the other way round.

A recent study published by Vlastakis/Dotsis/Markellos (2008) was able to show cross-firm arbitrage possibilities for football matches covering 26 countries and events. For the UK, this had already been shown by Dixon/Pope (2004).

So far, German football is some kind of terra incognita for studies dealing with betting lines. Only two (similar) papers about the possibilities for forecasting football results by using odds have been published, both by Quitzau (2005, 2006). These papers are distinguished by: (i) the absence of a formal background for the level of information and (ii) the fact that only 25 matchdays were analysed very simply.[5]

3.   THEORETICAL BACKGROUND

The general question is, on which factors does the winning probability of a professional football team depend? Next to the playing ability of the players involved (on an individual as well as a collective basis),[6] a factor of chance has to be considered. All influencing factors which are unknown until the beginning of the match are subsumed under the concept of chance. According to Quitzau (2005, 2006), this dimension can be divided into (i) luck and (ii) the form of the day. Luck covers aspects like decisions of the referee or changing weather conditions. Ex ante, 'luck' is equally distributed; ex post, differences can be recognized for both teams. In contrast, the form of the day refers to the team. It means that athletes are not able to achieve the same performance every day. Therefore, since any human being suffers from temporal fluctuations in physical and psychological condition, the team performance varies too.

The factor of playing ability depends on several aspects as well. First, the number of played matches in the season has to be considered. A team that has to play only 34 matches during a regular major league season in Germany is maybe fitter than a rival which has to play the same number of matches in the national league and additional matches in national cup tournaments, or international cups like the Champions League. The total number of obligatory matches cannot be assessed before the end of the season. That means the more successful a team is, the higher the number of matches it has to play.

Secondly, not only the form of the day, but also the form of the complete season has to be recognized. The long-term performance, which can be analysed over years, is known at every moment; in contrast, short- and mid-term performances can only be detected after several matches have been played.

The importance of whether a team plays in its own stadium or as a visiting guest has been the subject of some economic studies, like Sutter/Kocher (2004). In general, the home team has to be regarded as the stronger one, able to win more matches. Although the home field advantage has demonstrably decreased over the last decades (Heinrichs, 2008), it is still measurable and has to be considered in the estimation of winning probabilities.

Latently connected to the sports field factor, the surrounding conditions might influence the outcome and winning chances. Among surrounding conditions we include aspects such as the time of the match, weather conditions and the season of the year (which is strongly correlated to the weather conditions). Some of this information is known months before the match, but some becomes available only hours before the kick-off.

The third and final aspect that should be considered in this context is the team composition. This is affected by injuries as well as bans. Moreover, the team formation depends on the portfolio of the athletes who are contracted. The actual portfolio is constrained by (i) new players who have been contracted before the season, (ii) players who are not playing for the club any longer as they have been sold (or retired) and (iii) the majority of those who have not changed their contractual status. While information about changes in the squads is public, the problem is how to evaluate them: in team sports, manager and trainer face problems like moral hazard and adverse selection.[7] The question of the extent to which any new player is able to influence a team, or the extent to which the departure of an established player affects the team's performance can only be answered after several matches. Ex ante estimations are possible, but are affected by uncertainty.

A survey of these factors can be found in the appendix to this chapter. At first sight, it might be surprising that the financial strength of a club is not considered in this context. However, financial power does not influence performance directly, but indirectly (for example in the possibility of contracting new players).

To summarize, we can differentiate three categories of information:

- Aspects which are known before the season, such as the long-term performance of a team and past successes, which can be used as a benchmark. This long-term information level should be considered to be I_0.[8]
- Information influencing the winning probability and becoming obvious during a certain match (luck and form of the day), which cannot be used to forecast winning probabilities. In the sense of estimating these probabilities, luck and form of the day can be regarded as an error term ε.
- And finally the majority[9] of relevant information which becomes public during the current season. As this information depends on time, it can be depicted as $I(t)$.

In this context, we assume information to be public goods: once published, they are non-rival in consumption and non-exclusive. Moreover, any information is free; transaction costs are ignored. Based on these assumptions, Figure 6.1 can be derived.

The shape of $I(t)$ can differ in reality, but it should steadily increase during the season depending on time t. As a season progresses, additional data are revealed and team strength (regarding new players and so on) becomes more certain (Baryla *et al.*, 2007). According to Figure 6.1, we can postulate that $\partial I/\partial t > 0$ and $\partial^2 I/\partial t^2 < 0$, which follows the idea of a standard growth function, but is not strictly necessary in this context. A linear increase is also possible from a theoretical point of view, but some arguments support the shape as it is shown in Figure 6.1. The complete information level can be written as $I = I_0 + I(t) + \varepsilon$.

The quality of any estimation of winning probabilities has to depend on the availability of information formally given by the expression $Q(I(t))$, whereas I can be defined as a function of time $I(t)$.[10]

Postulating efficient utilization of the available information, the quality of the forecasts Q should improve during a season. Although we cannot give any precise statement about the shape of the infor-

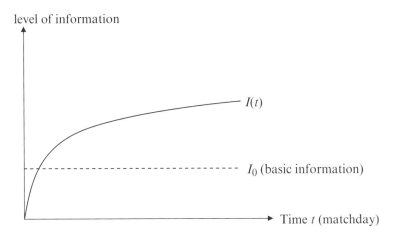

Figure 6.1   Level of information depending on time

mation level function (see above), it can be stated that the greater the information level is, the better and more precise any estimation can be: $\partial Q/\partial t > 0$. Starting at the level of I_0 (if something like a long-term information level is relevant), estimated winning probabilities of sports clubs playing in a round robin tournament have to become more precise in the course of time. Once again, $\partial^2 Q/\partial t^2 < 0$ is given intuitively, but cannot be proved. The model described so far implies that a secure estimation is impossible, as long as the error term ε is greater than zero.

Taking the betting market and its betting lines as a proxy for estimation quality on the basis of this model, we have to postulate an efficient market:

- when information is public and free of cost (see above) without any insider information,
- without any bettor bias,
- represented by bookmakers wishing to balance their books.

4.   DATA SET AND METHODS

In this section, the idea of an increasing quality in forecasting winning probabilities will be surveyed. The background to the study is a data set containing fixed[11] football odds from the 2003–04 season to the 2007–08 season. Within this period of five seasons, 1530 matches were played on 170 matchdays. The odds have been provided by *Oddset*, the public bookmaker, and contain three odds for every match: home victory (q_1), away victory (q_2) and draw (q_0).

The winning probabilities expected from the bookmaker can be derived from the odds by using the formula

$$\frac{\dfrac{1}{\dfrac{1}{q_1} + \dfrac{1}{q_2} + \dfrac{1}{q_0}}}{q_{1/2/3}}.$$

For the 2005–06 season, the odds for the first 11 matchdays are not fully available, so for this period the observation starts with matchday 12. Due to this, the number of matches considered is reduced to 1332. A numeric example will illustrate the relationship between odds and winning probabilities.

In the 2007–08 season, Schalke 04 had to play against Bayer Leverkusen. The odds were as follows: for a wager of one Euro, the bettor got €1.60 if Schalke won (home victory, q_1), €4.00 for Leverkusen winning (away victory, q_2) and €3.00 for a draw (q_0). The numerator can be derived as follows:

$$\frac{1}{\dfrac{1}{1.6} + \dfrac{1}{4.0} + \dfrac{1}{3.0}} = 0.8275.$$

The resulting probabilities are

- 51.72 per cent for a home victory,
- 20.69 per cent for an away victory and
- 27.59 per cent for a draw.

As expected, the probabilities add up to one. Some studies also account for the margin of the bookmaker, which is not necessary in this case, as the margin can be assumed to be identical for every result. For the matches in the observation period, we can assume a maximum winning probability of 76 per cent for the home team and 61 per cent for the away team, due to home advantage.

To analyse the impact of time on betting lines, we have to make sure that the betting market is efficient for the sample years, and the findings of other authors (for example Pankoff, 1968 and Pope/Peel, 1989; see section two) support this idea. General efficiency is given if there are no trading possibilities generating abnormal profits either (i) between the different outcomes of a single match (home victory, away victory, draw) or (ii) between the single matches of a matchday. As there is only one legal bookmaker available to German bettors, we do not have the option of analysing several companies.

i.   First the product of each single betting line and the corresponding winning probability were calculated. In the sense of efficiency, these payouts are identical for each possible result. Hence there are no trading possibilities between the three outcomes at a match level.

ii. The estimated payouts for the single matches were compared to the average of a complete matchday in step two. Only in 13 of 1332 cases was the difference greater than 1 per cent.[12] As a characteristic of *Oddset*, the bettor is not allowed to bet on single matches by using the 0-1-2 system, but has to bet on a specific result (for example 3:1). Furthermore, he can only place a bet on three or more games in a row. Apart from that, a fee of €0.30 has to be paid for each input. Given the characteristics explained above and the marginal differences of the estimated payouts, the idea of trading possibilities on a matchday level has to be rejected; market efficiency can be assumed.

First Approach

To study the influence of time on estimation quality, we group every nine matches played during one matchday in the *Bundesliga*. Every team has to play twice against all others, so there are 34 matchdays within one season. The analysis is based on five seasons, with a sum of 159 matchdays. The season of 2005–06, which is incomplete, causes the discrepancy in this calculation. The proxy for the exactitude of the estimations and their quality made by *Oddset* is represented by the sum of all nine actual probabilities. Assuming a matchday with only home victories, all probabilities for home victories are summed up. The points score indicates the ability to estimate the outcome of a match, over nine matches.

In a case where the favourite team, for example assessed with a winning probability of 65 per cent, wins the match, this will increase the points score. If the favourite loses the match and the underdog wins, the relevant probability of, for example, 15 per cent is considered in the score. The higher this score, the better was the ability to forecast the outcomes of the nine matches. For the affirmation of the model explained above – an increasing level of information results in an improved ability to estimate the winning probabilities – we expect an increasing points score during the season. For example for the tenth matchday in the 2007–08 season the score is given by Table 6.1.

If a bookmaker does not use his knowledge about the *Bundesliga*, he can use uniformly distributed probabilities. In this case, home victory, away victory and draw are expected to occur with a probability of 33.33 per cent each. The points score for a scenario like this would be 3 (= 9*1/3). In other words, it can be said that for a score of less than three, the bookmaker was beaten by chance: the effects of luck and 'form of the day' have influenced the outcome of the matches in such a strong way that the estimated winning probabilities were wrong in most cases.

Some of the core results of the analysis regarding the scores are summed up in Table 6.2. The slope of a linear regression for the scores depending on time is given once for the complete season, once for the first half and once for the second half of the season. These outcomes are surprising in more than one regard. First of all, for each season we can see scores of less than three, representing matchdays where the winning probabilities forecasted by the bookmakers were no better than chance. The minimum and maximum score of each season as well as the mean can be regarded to be quite constant.

Considering the slopes, the fact that all values are around zero has to be accepted. In four out of five cases, the slope (for the complete season) shows a positive sign, which accords with our theory of an increasing quality of forecasts. The negative slope in the 2005–06 season could be related to the missing data from the first 11 matchdays. The splitting of each season (except the season of 2005–06) and the calculation of separate slopes makes it possible to get an idea of the structure of information diffusion during a year. In this model, we expected a higher value for the slope at the beginning of the season, followed by a diminishing value in the long run. In fact, we are not able to confirm this assumption on the basis of four

Table 6.1   Matchday 10 in the 07/08 season

Home	Away	q_1	q_0	q_2	Result (goals)	p_1	p_0	p_2	Result	Score	Sum (of col.11)
Energie Cottbus	MSV Duisburg	1.90	2.85	**3.00**	1:2	0.4348	0.2899	0.2754	2	0.2754	
1. FC Nürnberg	Eintracht Frankfurt	**2.00**	2.80	2.80	5:1	0.4118	0.2941	0.2941	1	0.4118	
Bayer Leverkusen	Borussia Dortmund	1.75	**2.85**	3.40	2:2	0.4698	0.2884	0.2418	0	0.2884	
Hamburger SV	VfB Stuttgart	**1.85**	2.80	3.15	4:1	0.4448	0.2939	0.2613	1	0.4448	
Hansa Rostock	FC Schalke 04	3.40	**2.85**	1.75	1:1	0.2418	0.2884	0.4698	0	0.2884	
Werder Bremen	Hertha BSC	**1.40**	3.30	5.00	3:2	0.5868	0.2489	0.1643	1	0.5868	
VfL Bochum	Bayern Munich	5.20	3.20	**1.40**	1:2	0.1577	0.2563	0.5859	2	0.5859	
Hannover 96	VfL Wolfsburg	2.00	**2.80**	2.80	2:2	0.4118	0.2941	0.2941	0	0.2941	
Karlsruher SC	Arminia Bielefeld	1.70	**2.90**	3.50	0:0	0.4826	0.2829	0.2344	0	0.2829	**3.4586**

Note: Those betting odds which represent the result of the match are in bold, e.g., q_2 is bold if the guest team won the match.

Table 6.2   Key findings from the first approach

Season	03/04	04/05	05/06	06/07	07/08
Matchdays analysed	34	34	23	34	34
Max. score	4.1264	4.2702	3.8978	4.4213	4.3816
Min. score	2.8526	2.6807	2.8196	2.7316	2.4512
Mean	3.5552	3.4876	3.4480	3.3695	3.4715
Slope complete season	0.0074	0.0165	−0.0195	0.0079	0.0020
Slope first half	−0.0069	0.0169	–	0.0238	0.0057
Slope second half	0.0246	0.0040	–	0.0250	0.0186

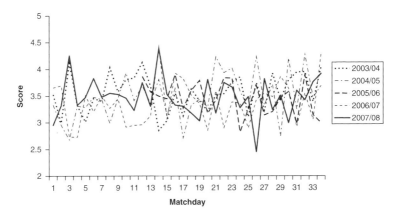

Figure 6.2   Score during the investigated seasons

observations. In general, the explanatory power of a linear regression used to analyse a time line of 34 observations has to be regarded as quite poor, which makes further analysis essential. Figure 6.2 covers all scores during the five seasons.

For advanced analysis, an autocorrelation analysis was used in the next step. The concerns relating to a linear regression are confirmed by the autocorrelation analysis. Obviously, the autocorrelation coefficient does not show any pattern and is slightly different from zero. Thus, we assume a white noise distribution![13] Hence, we have to rate the findings from the regression not to be significant, but stochastic!

Second Approach

In a second approach, we considered unequal matchdays. In some cases, it is quite easy for the bookmaker to estimate the winning probabilities, as the majority of single matches are unbalanced to a large extent (strong teams playing against weaker squads). In contrast, some matchdays contain mainly balanced matches without an odds-on favourite, which makes the estimation much more complicated.

For this reason, we summed up the nine highest winning probabilities of each matchday, representing the maximal score that can be achieved by the bookmaker. An example is given in Table 6.3. The mean of this maximal score is comparatively constant at 4.2 on a seasonal basis. In a second step, the spread between the maximal score and the actual score of each matchday has to be calculated. The smaller this spread, the better is the bookmaker's forecast. At best, the spread is zero, as all results are consistent with the bookmaker's expectation.[14] In the given example, the spread is 0.8388 (= 4.2974 − 3.4586).

The most important results are given in Table 6.4.

Once again, it is impossible to come to a general conclusion. Regarding the slope of a linear regression for four seasons (leaving out the incomplete 2005–06 season), a negative figure is shown in three cases. Decreasing spreads over the complete season accord with our hypothesis of an increasing estimation quality. But: the use of polynomial regressions (fourth grade) leads to different results. In particular, the 2004–05 season data reject the assumptions, as we find a u-shaped curve. In fact, this implies (i) an increasing estimation quality during the early matchdays and (ii) a decreasing quality from the 24th matchday on. In other cases, the regressions occur in a sinus-shape (for example in 2007–08); a decreasing trend is hardly in evidence.

Finally, an autocorrelation analyses for the spreads shows a white noise distribution once again.

5. DISCUSSION

The rejection of the hypothesis of an increasing quality in forecasting winning probabilities in the observation period must not

Table 6.3   *Consideration of the highest winning probabilities*

Home	Away	q_1	q_0	q_2	Result (goals)	p_1	p_0	p_2	Result	p_{max}	Max. Score
Energie Cottbus	MSV Duisburg	1.90	2.85	3.00	1:2	**0.4348**	0.2899	0.2754	2	0.4348	
1. FC Nürnberg	Eintracht Frankfurt	2.00	2.80	2.80	5:1	**0.4118**	0.2941	0.2941	1	0.4118	
Bayer Leverkusen	Borussia Dortmund	1.75	2.85	3.40	2:2	**0.4698**	0.2884	0.2418	0	0.4698	
Hamburger SV	VfB Stuttgart	1.85	2.80	3.15	4:1	**0.4448**	0.2939	0.2613	1	0.4448	
Hansa Rostock	FC Schalke 04	3.40	2.85	1.75	1:1	0.2418	0.2884	**0.4698**	0	0.4698	
Werder Bremen	Hertha BSC	1.40	3.30	5.00	3:2	**0.5868**	0.2489	0.1643	1	0.5861	
VfL Bochum	Bayern Munich	5.20	3.20	1.40	1:2	0.1577	0.2563	**0.5859**	2	0.5859	
Hannover 96	VfL Wolfsburg	2.00	2.80	2.80	2:2	**0.4118**	0.2941	0.2941	0	0.4118	
Karlsruher SC	Arminia Bielefeld	1.70	2.90	3.50	0:0	**0.4826**	0.2829	0.2344	0	0.4826	**4.2974**

Note: Numbers in bold are the maximum of p_0, p_1, p_2.

Table 6.4   Key findings from the second approach

Season	03/04	04/05	05/06	06/07	07/08
Matchdays analysed	34	34	23	34	34
Max. spread	1.3328	1.7780	1.2912	1.6109	1.7272
Min. spread	0.0000	0.0804	0.2562	0.1624	0.0000
Mean	0.6491	0.7926	0.8254	0.8276	0.7298
Slope complete season	−0.0069	−0.0050	0.0143	−0.0079	0.0013
Slope first half	0.0051	−0.0141	–	−0.0254	0.0009
Slope second half	−0.0245	0.0260	–	−0.0088	−0.0150

be generalized. The data set is obviously too small to generate robust findings. More research, especially the consideration of other countries, is necessary to end up with a generalized result. Finally, the assumptions regarding the model (efficient betting markets, no insider information, no biases) are quite strict. However, the assumption that forecasting winning probabilities in professional football cannot improve during a season, could have several interesting reasons, which should be explained.

First of all, it is possible, that *Oddset* and its analysts are not able to transform information in an appropriate way into winning probabilities. As this bookmaker is known as a major player in Germany's betting market, this assumption should be rejected.[15] Moreover, betting lines are known to be unbiased predictors of actual game outcomes (Gandar *et al.*, 1988 and section 2 of this chapter). The second, and more provocative possibility, is that the outcome of a football match depends on chance to a large extent. This outcome has already been mentioned (for the case of the *Bundesliga*) by Quitzau (2005, 2006), who considered betting odds too, but chose a slightly different, much simpler approach. The major influence of chance at every stage of a season is tangent to some aspects of the regulation and organization of a league. If the probability of a single team winning a match cannot be forecasted, this implies (i) a high uncertainty of outcome[16] and (ii) the fact that the financial options of a team are not closely linked to performance (on a single match level). The problem is to define the correct terms for conclusions like this. There is hardly any doubt that the financial power of a club influences human capital equipment and long-term team success. However, in the short run, regarding a single season or a few years, aspects like form of the day (form of the season?) seem to play an important role. The influence of sport leagues as a factor in decreasing consumer interest could be a result of chance in the short run.

6. OUTLOOK

This chapter shows the role of information in the estimation of winning probabilities in professional football. Based on the assumption of efficient markets in sport betting (which is necessary for a complete theoretical background) and an increasing information level during a football season, we tried to show an increasing quality of forecasts. On a data set containing the odds for five seasons, this increase could not be verified in a simple time row analysis.

Further research should concentrate on a similar analysis for other countries and/or other disciplines; in particular, disciplines offering longer series than only 34 matchdays are expected to generate more robust findings.

ACKNOWLEDGEMENTS

The authors are indebted to an anonymous referee and the editor for their useful comments.

NOTES

1. We are using the term *football* as equivalent to the American *soccer*. Football in a US sense is prefixed by *American*.
2. This assumption is shared by Gandar *et al.* (1988).
3. In the UK a draw is denoted by 3.
4. The only exceptions are so-called handicap bets: the bettor uses the standard 0-1-2 system but the team which is known to be weaker in performance during the season is assumed to have an advantage of one or two goals.
5. More information about these papers can be found in the course of the article.
6. The playing ability of a whole football team is known to be more than just the addition of the talent of 11 athletes. Depending on the team-specific human capital of each player, we have to consider a team performance which is much higher than the sum of the individual talents.
7. Further information on these aspects of professional sport can be found in Benz (2007) and Kahn (2004).
8. The influence of long-term information in the given context on short-term

performance and match results is anything but clear and should not be over-estimated. It is influenced, for example, by rule changes (such as the introduction of the three-point rule), player transfers (Baryla *et al.*, 2007) and promotion and relegation. For a team playing in the major league for the first year, the long-term information is close to zero; a precise assessment seems to be impossible. In fact, long-term performance information could be something that only exists in the minds of bettors, but is not relevant for estimating winning probabilities. As I_0 is of minor importance in the given context, we pass on further submissions.

9. The term *majority* in this context refers to the quantitative dimension and does not make any judgements on the qualitative importance of single factors.

10. Neither the error term nor the long-term information are influenced by time; they have to be regarded as constant during a season.

11. Beside the question of whether the bookmakers are offering bets on spreads or only on the victory itself, two other types of bets have to be distinguished. In the first case, the betting odds are variable and can change, for example, if any information is made public within a few days or even hours of the match. In the second case, we are speaking of fixed odds. The bookmaker sets them such that they reflect his subjective estimated probability relating to the outcome. In this case, the bettor will have more information concerning the 'form' of the athletes than the bookmaker (Pope/Peel, 1989).

12. One possible reason for these minimal spreads might be the fact that *Oddset* represents a public monopoly.

13. For further information about white noise distribution, see for example Schlittgen/Streitberg (2001).

14. In reality, this case can be disregarded as it occurs only twice during the observation period.

15. An idea which has been ignored so far, is that *Oddset* and its experts are able to transform information into correct betting lines (from a technical point of view), but have a different agenda. Instead of balancing the book to eliminate risk, exploiting known bettor biases such as the favourite-longshot bias could be the major aim. Levitt (2004) introduced the thesis of a non-risk-eliminating bookmaker to explain inefficient betting markets, and a few recent studies (see for example Paul/Weinbach, 2007, 2008) dealt with that question. A test for the German market during the observation period is not possible as the necessary data set (what sums have been bet on which result) is not public. A formal request directed to *Oddset* was rejected.

16. For more information about the influence of the uncertainty of outcome in team sports see Rottenberg (1956), Czarnitzki/Stadtmann (2002) and Forrest/Simmons (2006).

REFERENCES

Baryla, Edward A., Richard A. Borghesi, William H. Dare and Steven A. Dennis (2007), 'Learning, price formation and the early season bias in the NBA', *Finance Research Letters*, **4**, 155–164.

Benz, Men-Andri (2007), *Strategies in Markets for Experience and Credence Goods*, Wiesbaden, Germany: Deutscher Universitäts-Verlag.

Brailsford, Timothy J., Philip K. Gray, Steven A. Easton and Steven F.

Gray (1995), 'The efficiency of Australian football betting markets', *Australian Journal of Management*, **20** (2), 167–195.

Brown, Kenneth H. and Fred J. Abraham (2002) 'Testing market efficiency in Major League Baseball over-under betting market', *Journal of Sports Economics*, **3** (4), 311–319.

Cain, Michael, David Law and David A. Peel (2000), 'The favorite-longshot bias and market efficiency in UK football betting', *Scottish Journal of Political Economy*, **47** (1), 25–36.

Czarnitzki, Dirk and Georg Stadtmann (2002), 'Uncertainty of outcome versus reputation: empirical evidence for the First German Football Division', *Empirical Economics*, **22**, 101–112.

Dare, William H. and A. Steven Holland (2004), 'Efficiency in the NFL betting market: modifying and consolidating research methods', *Applied Economics*, **36**, 9–15.

Daumann, Frank and Markus Breuer (2008), 'Zur Neuordnung des Lotteriemarktes in Deutschland', *ORDO*, **59**, 287–312.

Dixon, Mark J. and Stuart G. Coles (1997), 'Modelling association football scores and inefficiencies in the football betting market', *Applied Statistics*, **46** (2), 265–280.

Dixon, Mark J. and Peter F. Pope (2004), 'The value of statistical forecasts in the UK association football betting market', *International Journal of Forecasting*, **20**, 697–711.

Fama, Eugene F. (1970), 'Efficient capital markets: a review of theory and empirical work', *The Journal of Finance*, **25** (2), 383–417.

Fama, Eugene F. (1991), 'Efficient capital markets: II', *The Journal of Finance*, **46** (5), 1575–1617.

Fama, Eugene F. (1998), 'Market efficiency, long-term returns, and behavioural finance', *The Journal of Financial Economics*, **49**, 283–306.

Forrest, David, John Goddard and Robert Simmons (2005), 'Odds-setters as forecasters: the case of English football', *International Journal of Forecasting*, **21**, 551–564.

Forrest, David and Robert Simmons (2006), 'New issues in attendance demand: the case of the English Football League', *Journal of Sports Economics*, **7** (3), 247–266.

Gandar, John M., Richard A. Zuber and William H. Dare (2000), 'The search for informed traders in the totals betting market for national Basketball Association games', *Journal of Sports Economics*, **1** (2), 177–186.

Gandar, John M., Richard A. Zuber and R. Stafford Johnson (2004), 'Reexamination of the efficiency of the betting market on National Hockey League games', *Journal of Sports Economics*, **5** (2), 152–168.

Gandar, John M., Richard A. Zuber, R. Stafford Johnson and William H. Dare (2002), 'Re-examining the betting market on Major League Baseball games: is there a reverse favourite-longshot bias?' *Applied Economics*, **34** (10), 1309–1317.

Gandar, John M., Richard A. Zuber, Thomas O'Brien and Ben Russo (1988), 'Testing rationality in the point spread betting market', *The Journal of Finance*, **43** (4), 995–1008.

Gray, Philip K. and Steven F. Gray (1997), 'Testing market efficiency: evidence from the NFL sports betting market', *The Journal of Finance*, **52** (4), 1725–1737.

Heinrichs, Eva (2008), *Mythos Heimvorteil*, Dortmund: Dortmund University of Technology.

Kahn, Lawrence M. (2004), 'The sports business as a labor market laboratory', in Scott R. Rosner and Kenneth L. Shropshire (eds), *The Business of Sports*, Sudbury, MA, USA: Jones and Bartlett, pp. 242–251.

Levitt, Steven D. (2004), 'Why are gambling markets organized so differently from financial markets?' *The Economic Journal*, **114**, 223–246.

Pankoff, Lyn D. (1968), 'Market efficiency and football betting', *The Journal of Business*, **41**, 203–214.

Paul, Rodney J. and Andrew P. Weinbach (2005), 'The overbetting of large favorites and the "hot hand"', *Journal of Sports Economics*, **6** (4), 390–400.

Paul, Rodney J. and Andrew P. Weinbach (2007), 'Does sportsbook.com set point-spreads to maximize profits? Tests of the Levitt model of sportsbook behavior', *Journal of Prediction Markets*, **1** (3), 209–218.

Paul, Rodney J. and Andrew P. Weinbach (2008), 'Price setting in the NBA gambling market: tests of the Levitt model on sportsbook behavior', *International Journal of Sports Finance*, **3**, 137–145.

Paul, Rodney J., Andrew P. Weinbach and Chris J. Weinbach (2003), 'Fair bets and profitability in college football gambling', *Journal of Economics and Finance*, **27** (2), 236–242.

Paul, Rodney J., Andrew P. Weinbach and Mark Wilson (2004), 'Efficient markets, fair bets, and profitability in NBA totals 1995–96 to 2001–02', *The Quarterly Review of Economics and Finance*, **44**, 624–632.

Pope, Peter F. and David A. Peel (1989), 'Information, prices and efficiency in a fixed-odds betting market', *Economica*, **56**, 323–341.

Quitzau, Jörn (2005), *Faktor Zufall als Spielverderber: zur Prognostizierbarkeit von Fussballergebnissen: Wettmärkte als effizienter Informationslieferant*, Deutsche Bank Research Note, No. 18, Frankfurt/Main: Deutsche Bank.

Quitzau, Jörn (2006), 'Zufall als Spielgestalter', *Wirtschaftswissenschaftliches Studium*, **35** (4), 200–205.

Rottenberg, Simon (1956), 'The baseball players' labor market', *Journal of Political Economy*, **64**, 242–258.

Schlittgen, Rainer and Bernd H.J. Streitberg (2001), *Zeitreihenanalyse*, 9th edn, Munich: Oldenbourg.

Stefani, Raymond T. (1983), 'Observed betting tendencies and suggested betting strategies for European football pools', *The Statistician*, **32**, 319–329.

Sutter, Matthias and Martin G. Kocher (2004), 'Favoritism of agents: the case of referees' home bias', *Journal of Economic Psychology*, **25**, 461–469.

Vergin, Roger C. and Michael Scriabin (1978), 'Winning strategies for wagering on National Football League games', *Management Science*, **24**, 809–818.

Vlastakis, Nikolaos, George Dotsis and Raphael N. Markellos (2008),

How efficient is the European football betting market? Evidence from arbitrage and trading strategies, working paper, available at: http://ssrn.com/abstract=984469, accessed 4 January 2010.

Woodland, Linda M. and Bill M. Woodland (2001), 'Market efficiency and profitable wagering in the National Hockey League: can bettors score on longshots?' *Southern Economic Journal*, **67** (4), 983–995.

Zuber, Richard A., John M. Gandar and Benny D. Bowers (1985), 'Beating the spread: testing the efficiency of the gambling market for National Football League games', *Journal of Political Economy*, **93** (4), 800–806.

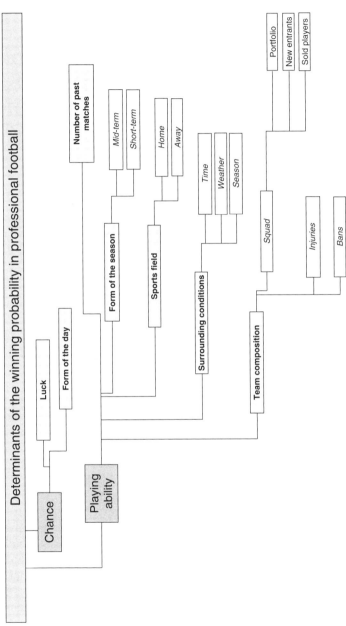

Figure 6A.1   Determinants of the winning probability in professional football

7. Guessing who wins or predicting the exact score: does it make any difference in terms of the demand for football pools?

Jaume García, Levi Pérez and Plácido Rodríguez[1]

INTRODUCTION

The Spanish State Lotteries and Gaming (*Loterías y Apuestas del Estado* – LAE), a government organisation reporting to the Ministry of Economy and Finance via the State Secretary for Finance and Budgets, controls most legal sports betting in Spain. Sport betting consists of pools and other competitions for forecasting the results of sports events. Despite Spain's enthusiasm for football, legal sports betting in relation to football is largely limited to people gambling on the outcome of professional football matches through football pools.[1]

As in the case of lotteries, the introduction of football pools in the gambling market could be explained in terms of the desire of governments to identify a new source of revenue. Furthermore, the exceptional importance of this gambling industry in Spain lies in the scope of its economic and social benefits; generally speaking, the funds obtained have been used to further promote sporting activities. Thus the LAE seeks to maximise revenue for the state or its nominated organisations (such as those promoting sports or the professional football teams). As revenues are a fixed proportion of sales, football pools managers should be motivated to maximise sales. To see if revenue-maximising game designs have been chosen, we need to look at the determinants of participation, which include the price, the size of the prize pool and the difficulty of the game (that is, the probability of winning the top prize, known as a jackpot).

On the other hand, we also consider the relevance of the composition of betting coupons, meaning the teams included in them (it is a characteristic of the good to be consumed, which is different in each fixture and may have a significant effect on participation), to account for the importance of the 'illusion of control' in football pools where bettors use their knowledge of football teams to try to correctly guess the results of the designated matches. Even though the empirical research into how football pools are run or how they should be designed is limited, pools sales have been found to be influenced by game characteristics such as price, prizes and the composition of the coupon (Forrest, 1999; García and Rodriguez, 2007; García *et al.*, 2008).

Since LAE manages Spanish football pools by means of two different modes of gambling, including particular rules, structure and operation (for example, choosing the final result or predicting the exact score of some football games), we are not only interested in analysing how all these features affect sales of football pools, but we are also concerned about whether their effect has a different sign and/or size depending on the particular game design.

In order to study the effects of all the parameters mentioned above on football pools sales it is necessary to model their effects on participation. Since football pools share some characteristics with lotto games (in that both are pari-mutuel games), previous research has dealt with a demand model based on the same economic framework used in empirical models that study lotto demand: the effective price model and the jackpot model. The aim of this chapter then is to analyse the determinants of demand for football pools in Spain, (1) focusing on statistical issues concerned with the main economic variable behind the empirical evidence and (2) dealing with the different effects of the main covariates on the demand for football pools according to the considered mode of betting. Finally, the results are expected to evaluate the effect of other potential determinants of sales, such as addiction and seasonality, and to have important implications for how each game should be operated to increase demand.

FOOTBALL POOLS IN SPAIN

Football pools (*La Quiniela*) were introduced in Spain in the 1946–47 season by LAE, which is also responsible for operating the

Lotería Nacional (a passive lottery game), with several high payouts, low odds lotto games and some lottery-type games related to horse racing. The pools have long occupied an important place in the Spanish gambling market. For many years the demand for a long-odds, high-prize gambling product was met by this game.

For several years *La Quiniela*, together with the National Lottery and the Spanish National Organisation for the Blind lottery (a daily draw), were the only three legal betting games available in Spain. The importance of this gambling industry delayed the introduction of a competing lotto game. However, when it was eventually introduced in 1985, the impact on the pools was severe. As mentioned in García and Rodríguez (2007), football pools sales fell by nearly 80 per cent between 1985 and 1990, and this can largely be explained by the appearance of *La Primitiva* (a 6/49 lotto game) on the Spanish gambling market.[2] The pools industry response has included several changes to the game design and the introduction of a new game. Now football pools in Spain include two different games: *La Quiniela* and *El Quinigol*.

The main game is *La Quiniela*,[3] where each bet is composed of fifteen matches that correspond, in general, to Spanish First and Second Division teams. Bettors can choose the final result of each match from among three alternatives: home win (1), draw (X) and away win (2). To win the maximum prize, bettors must correctly guess the results of all fifteen matches included in the coupon. If the main prize is not won, it is rolled over to the following week. Lower prizes are awarded to those correctly guessing 10, 11, 12, 13 or 14 results. It must be noted that if the prize per bet for those who correctly guessed ten is less than €1, the prize is not paid out, and the funds for this category roll over into the next fixture. Tickets cost €0.50 and can be bought at any of the widely available local state lottery shops throughout Spain. Bettors can ask for a lucky dip, but there is a two-column minimum entry fee of €1 for a bet.[4]

El Quinigol, a football betting pool based on the Spanish football league, was introduced in 1998 to coincide with the Football World Cup in France.[5] The name is derived from the fact that bettors are required to predict the number of goals that will be scored by the teams involved. Each bet costs €1 and includes six matches, which naturally involve a total of twelve football teams. There are four sections for each team. You have to mark (with an X) the section that corresponds to the number of goals you believe each team is

Figure 7.1   A coupon for La Quiniela

going to score. For example, if you mark the '1' section with an X, you are indicating that the team will score just one goal. To win a prize, bettors have to correctly guess at least two of the six matches included. The maximum prize is won by those who guess the exact result for each of the six matches. When there is no winner in the top category, the pool prize for this category rolls over. If the prize per bet allocated to the winners of the fifth category (that is, two matches correctly guessed) is less than €1, the winners of this category receive no prize, and the accumulated funds for this category roll over.

The take-out rate on both games is 45 per cent – which is less than with UK football pools and on par with Spanish lotteries – and payouts are pari-mutuel, so prizes are a percentage of the total revenue.

To better understand how to make a bet on Spanish football pools, the current coupons for both *La Quiniela* and *El Quinigol* are shown in Figures 7.1 and 7.2 respectively. In addition, Table 7.1 lists the current arrangements for each of the two games.

Besides establishing strong links with football, football pool funds have also been set up to channel significant investment into football-related social causes. A Spanish Royal Decree of 20 February 1998 established the current distribution of football pool revenues. The

Figure 7.2   A coupon for El Quinigol

Spanish Professional Football League (LFP) receives 10 per cent,[6] the National Council of Sports gets 1 per cent and 10.98 per cent goes to the provincial governments to promote social activities and sport facilities. The Public Exchequer takes 23 per cent of total revenues once the administration and distribution expenses have been taken into account.

THE ECONOMICS OF THE DEMAND FOR FOOTBALL POOLS

As football pools share some characteristics with lotto games (in that both are pari-mutuel games), previous research has dealt with the demand models based on the same economic framework and using the same empirical models as in the lotto demand literature. Thus, we follow the most common approaches in the empirical literature on the demand for lotto, assuming that sales are dependent on either the effective price (Cook and Clotfelter, 1993; Gulley and Scott, 1993; Scott and Gulley, 1995; Walker, 1998; Farrell and Walker, 1999; Farrell et al., 1999; Forrest et al., 2000) – defined as the difference between the entry fee and the expected value of a prize for a

Table 7.1   Current rules of Spanish football pools

	La Quiniela	El Quinigol
Number of football games included	15	6
Ticket price (€)	0.5	1
Take-out rate	0.45	0.45
Prize categories	6	5
Share of the prize pool *		
Jackpot	10% + rollover	10% + rollover
2nd category	12 %	9 %
3rd category	8 %	8 %
4th category	8 %	8 %
5th category	8 %	20 %
6th category	9 %	–

Note: * Percentage of total revenues.

single bet – or the jackpot (Forrest *et al.*, 2002) – a term referring to the size of the top prize.

The principal sources of variability in the data (which extend over 130 fixtures in the case of *La Quiniela* and over 160 fixtures for *El Quinigol*) are both the rollover of the jackpot from one fixture to the next and the composition of the list of matches included in the corresponding coupon. The first component induces variation in the top prize as well as in the expected return and allows us to estimate a demand function for each game from the correlation between variations in bet sales for a game and changes in either the jackpot or the effective price of that game. The latter component is expected to affect participation strongly.

Following Farrell and Walker (1999), the expected value (*ev*) of holding a football pool bet, assuming a single prize pool and a unit price to simplify the presentation, is calculated as follows:

$$ev = [r / q + (1 - \tau)] (1 - \pi) \tag{7.1}$$

where *r* is the amount rolled over from a previous fixture without winners, *q* is the total number of bets sold, τ is the take-out rate (the share of the revenues that is not distributed in prizes) and π is the probability of there being no winning bet. This expression is adjusted

Table 7.2   *Definition of the price, the expected value and the jackpot of a bet*

Game	Price	Expected Value (*ev*)	Jackpot (*j*)
La Quiniela	€0.50	$ev = [\,p_{10}\,0.09i + 0.24i + p_{14}0.12 + p_{15}(0.1i + r)]/q$	$j = 0.22i + r$
El Quinigol	€1	$ev = [0.25i + p_6(0.1i + r) + p_{p5 > 1}0.2i]/q$	$j = 0.1i + r$

Notes: * i = total revenue (number of bets times the price of a single bet); r = the rollover; q = sales; p_{10}, p_{14}, p_{15} = probability of correctly guessing 10, 14 and 15 matches in *La Quiniela*; p_6 = probability of correctly guessing 6 matches in *El Quinigol*; $p_{p5 > 1}$ = in *El Quinigol*, probability of the prize per bet devoted to winners of the fifth category (2 matches correctly guessed) being more than €1 (0.94375).

to reflect that not all of the prize money is available to the jackpot pool. Adding the contribution of the smaller prizes to the expected value of a bet is straightforward to the extent that it can be reasonably assumed that all other prize funds are paid out.

In a similar way, we define the jackpot (j) as:

$$j = (1 - \tau)\,q + r \qquad (7.2)$$

Table 7.2 reports the entry fee for each game over the sample period and the full formulae employed in the calculations of both the expected value and the jackpot. Calculations take into account the separate rules of each game.

The game design has an obvious influence on the probability of a bet being a winner. For instance, in the case of lotto (6/49), the probability of having a winning ticket is known in advance (1:14 m). However, this is not the case in football pools. The probability ex ante of winning a football pool will change depending on the particular signs or predictions for each match. However, we will assume that there is an ex ante probability of having a winning bet, which is constant for all bets. Thus, in order to calculate the expected prize of a *La Quiniela* bet, we have to weight prizes associated with 10, 14 and 15 correct guesses[7] by the probability of having at least one winner of this prize because if there is no winner, the prize rolls over. These probabilities are approximated by the proportion of fixtures with winners of the prizes of 10, 14 or 15 correct guesses during the whole sample period (0.94253, 0.93678 and 0.81203, respectively).

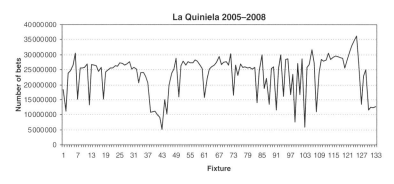

Figure 7.3   Sales of La Quiniela *over time*

The same was applied to the prize for those who guessed six correctly in *El Quinigol,* so we approximate the probability that the amount for this prize does not roll over, p_6, in the same way as we did before (0.125).

Since the effective price model and the jackpot model have different implications in terms of both bettors' behaviour and changes in the structure of prizes, we will compare the performance of both models as an additional objective of this chapter. This follows an approach similar to that of Forrest *et al.* (2002).

DATA

Using all fixture data from the seasons between 2005–2006 and 2007–2008,[8] we estimate a demand equation for each game in order to identify the main economic determinant of sales. Furthermore, we pay special attention to other factors affecting variation in participation. These features have some relevant implications on the demand for football pools because the effect of changing either the composition of the list of matches in each bet or the design of the game will alter sales depending on the game.

With regard to sales, Figures 7.3 and 7.4 show the number of tickets sold for each game on a fixture-by-fixture basis. We can observe substantial variability in spending on both games, both within a certain game as well as among games. Thus bets range from between 5 million and 36 million in the case of *La Quiniela*. The average sales were approximately 23 million bets throughout

Figure 7.4   Sales of El Quinigol *over time*

the sample period. In *El Quinigol*, over 200 000 bets were placed on average with a maximum of approximately 471 000 bets. Since the price of a ticket and the prize structure remain fixed over time in both games, this high variability in sales should be explained by changes in the expected value of tickets due to variation in participation (expected to be directly affected by the composition of the list of football matches included in each coupon) and rollovers.[9]

As we mentioned before, there is the issue of 'illusion of control' which is probably more important than in lotto games (Forrest *et al.*, 2002). Thus, we think that football pools are different because bettors are knowledgeable about the teams involved in each coupon. Therefore, we expect that the teams included in each bet represent a decisive determinant of participation and act as a key variable of football pools management. This is controlled for by introducing a dummy variable for the absence of either First Division teams or Second Division teams in each coupon.[10]

We also wish to control for the effect of other potential determinants of sales such as addiction, seasonality and whether it is a weekend fixture or not. Thus, as suggested by Walker (1998), amongst others, we consider one lag of the dependent variable to control for habit persistence in football pools. We also include a trend (fixture number) and its square to account for any secular changes in people's preferences for playing. Interest in some betting markets fades over time as boredom and disillusion set in.

Finally, given that we are dealing with time series data, we need to control for seasonality effects. We do this by introducing dummy

Table 7.3   Descriptive statistics: La Quiniela *and* El Quinigol

	Mean	Standard Deviation
Number of bets per fixture (thousands)		
La Quiniela	23 451.204	6 498.550
El Quinigol	206.779	67.641
Effective price (€)		
La Quiniela	0.225	0.035
El Quinigol	0.488	0.045
Jackpot (thousands €)		
La Quiniela	3 125.282	1 701.345
El Quinigol	119.240	77.575
Fixtures without Spanish First Division teams		
La Quiniela	0.165	0.373
El Quinigol	0.281	0.451
Fixtures without Spanish Second Division teams		
La Quiniela	0.023	0.149
El Quinigol	0.956	0.205
Midweek fixtures		
La Quiniela	0.060	0.239
El Quinigol	0.219	0.415

variables corresponding to months,[11] Easter week and midweek fixtures and the first two fixtures of the season. Summary statistics are reported in Table 7.3.

EMPIRICAL FINDINGS

Estimates are expected to preliminarily evaluate whether the revenue-maximising design has been chosen and to analyse how the main determinants of football pools demand affect sales depending on the game.

Since football pools are pari-mutuel, the amount devoted to prizes depends on sales, so both the effective price and the jackpot are endogenous to the demand function. As a result, we could not estimate our models using ordinary least squares. Thus, we estimated both models by instrumental variables (iv) using the rollover and its square to instrument both variables. This technique is appropriate because they are correlated with both variables and because they are clearly exogenous variables that have been determined previously.

Modelling results are displayed in Table 7.4. Although both games are related to football, some differences are expected to be found according to the different structures and operations. Thus, even though strong habit effects are captured by a highly significant coefficient on the lagged dependent variable, it should be noted that the effect of habit persistence on football pools sales is stronger in the case of *El Quinigol*. This could be explained in terms of individuals betting on the exact score being more loyal and skilled bettors than those just guessing which team wins. Although this is not apparent from Figure 7.3, the linear trend term is positive in the case of *La Quiniela*, which suggests increasing popularity for this game. This coefficient is negative in the case of *El Quinigol*, indicating that players' enthusiasm for this game is decreasing. However, since the coefficient on trend is negative and the coefficient on trend square is positive, the rate of decay decreases as the fixtures go by, all else being equal.

As in previous papers dealing with Spanish football pools (García and Rodríguez, 2007; García *et al.*, 2008) and according to the results in Table 7.4, we can conclude that for both games, the jackpot model fits the data better than the effective price model in terms of the adjusted R^2. However, we know that the comparison of this measure for the models is not a formal test of which model is the best specification because the models are not nested, but in any case we think that this rough comparison gives convincing information about how well both models explain what has happened with football pool sales.

Revenue maximisation occurs when further changes to the prize are just offset by changes in the sales quantity (implying a price elasticity of −1). To see if the revenue-maximising design has been chosen, we need to examine the price elasticity of demand. Apart from price, the determinant of revenues, participation and sales also depends on the take-out rate (that is, the share of revenues that is not distributed through prizes) and on the game design (in particular, on the probability of winning the jackpot).

We found that the long-run elasticity of sales[12] with respect to the 'price' is close to −1 for *El Quinigol* (−0.972), implying revenue

Table 7.4   Parameter estimates and p-values

	La Quiniela		El Quinigol	
Effective price (log)	–0.165	–	–0.482	–
	(0.000)	–	(0.001)	–
Jackpot (log)	–	0.132	–	0.052
	–	(0.000)	–	(0.001)
Bets lagged 1 week (log)	0.126	0.110	0.504	0.488
	(0.000)	(0.000)	(0.000)	(0.000)
Trend	0.001	0.001	–0.007	–0.006
	(0.000)	(0.000)	(0.000)	(0.000)
Trend^2	–	–	3.56e–05	3.27e–05
	–	–	(0.000)	(0.000)
No Spanish First	–0.621	–0.533	–0.176	–0.160
Division teams	(0.000)	(0.000)	(0.000)	(0.000)
No Spanish Second	–0.420	–0.367	–	–
Division teams	(0.000)	(0.000)	–	–
January	0.319	0.270	0.342	0.314
	(0.000)	(0.000)	(0.002)	(0.002)
February	0.393	0.336	0.368	0.339
	(0.000)	(0.000)	(0.001)	(0.001)
March	0.379	0.326	0.390	0.357
	(0.000)	(0.000)	(0.000)	(0.000)
April	0.358	0.312	0.342	0.335
	(0.000)	(0.000)	(0.003)	(0.002)
May	0.232	0.203	0.255	0.242
	(0.001)	(0.001)	(0.018)	(0.015)
June	0.212	0.180	0.432	0.400
	(0.003)	(0.003)	(0.000)	(0.000)
July	–	–	–	–
	–	–	–	–
August	–	–	–	–
	–	–	–	–
September	0.292	0.246	0.382	0.345
	(0.000)	(0.000)	(0.000)	(0.001)
October	0.410	0.354	0.416	0.394
	(0.000)	(0.000)	(0.000)	(0.000)
November	0.439	0.377	0.356	0.341
	(0.000)	(0.000)	(0.001)	(0.001)
December	0.381	0.326	0.366	0.334
	(0.000)	(0.000)	(0.001)	(0.001)
Midweek	–0.611	–0.525	–0.234	–0.222
	(0.000)	(0.000)	(0.000)	(0.000)

Table 7.4   (continued)

	La	Quiniela	El	Quinigol
Easter week	−0.040	−0.043	−0.073	−0.073
	(0.382)	(0.274)	(0.335)	(0.293)
Fixture 1	−	−	−	−
	−	−	−	−
Fixture 2	−0.063	−0.058	0.053	0.053
	(0.028)	(0.019)	(0.249)	(0.205)
Constant	13.510	13.488	3.476	5.857
	(0.000)	(0.000)	(0.000)	(0.000)
Adjusted R²	**0.947**	**0.961**	**0.770**	**0.807**
N	**132**	**132**	**159**	**159**

Notes: All the economic variables are in real terms.
Dependent variable: (log) Number of bets sold for each game.

maximisation. For *La Quiniela*, however, elasticity is, in absolute value terms, significantly lower (−0.189), implying that this game design could be changed to increase sales revenues. Thus, decreasing the effective price of *La Quiniela* would lead to an increase in its sales because its effective price elasticity is inelastic. In this case, the LAE could increase the effective price to maximise net revenue from this game. In fact, the effective price could be increased by raising the price of a unit bet, by reducing the odds of winning the jackpot (thereby increasing the difficulty of the game) or by increasing the take-out.

With respect to jackpot elasticity, it is quite different in the short run for the two games considered, being positive and significant and showing the importance of the effect of rollovers on sales.

It seems that bettors in *La Quiniela* are more influenced by changes in the jackpot than people playing *El Quinigol*. This confirms the result we had previously mentioned concerning the fact that the jackpot model is preferred over the effective price model and could also be catching a different profile of player depending on the game and be affected by the difference in the difficulty of each game. Thus, in the short run, bets in *El Quinigol* are quite sensitive to changes in the effective price instead of increases in the jackpot. These results emphasise the impact on sales of different specifications of the structure of the game and prizes.

As mentioned in the introduction, we are also interested in analysing the effect of the list of matches included in the coupon on the demand for football pools. According to the estimation results, the impact of the absence of Spanish First Division teams on the coupon implies a different reduction in sales depending on the game. The evidence in Table 7.4 illustrates that not including First Division teams on the coupon has a relatively important (negative) impact on sales of *La Quiniela*[13] but a quite small effect on *El Quinigol*. This different effect on sales could be explained in terms of the structure and rules of each game. When *El Quinigol* was introduced, the coupon included either National Teams or teams from the European Champions League, so bettors in this game are used to betting on Spanish and non-Spanish teams. Thus, the effect of the absence of teams from the Spanish First Division is less pronounced for *El Quinigol* than for *La Quiniela*.

Given that we have time series data for the fixtures, we considered some dummy variables to capture seasonal patterns in the evolution of sales. Thus, the first fixtures, which correspond to the end of August or the beginning of September, have smaller sales in both games. Additionally, some 'fatigue' is evident among bettors as the season progresses. However, sales of *El Quinigol* are unusually high in June. This is because of the introduction of several 'special fixtures' in *El Quinigol* at the end of both the 2005–2006 season and the 2007–2008 season, coinciding with the 2006 FIFA World Cup and the 2008 UEFA European Football Championship, respectively.

The midweek features also cause a substantial reduction in sales, but this decrease is quite different between *La Quiniela* and *El Quinigol*. Again, it could be explained in terms of the significantly higher number of midweek fixtures (approximately 22 per cent) in *El Quinigol*, where bettors are used to betting on games from the European Champions League that take place in the middle of the week (both Tuesdays and Wednesdays).

CONCLUDING REMARKS

We have modelled sales of football pools in Spain by using separate equations for each of the modes of betting. Using data corresponding to the fixtures from three consecutive seasons, we estimated a demand equation in an attempt to identify whether the effective price or the jackpot better capture the evolution of sales. Although these two variables have a different effect on sales depending on the game, we concluded that the jackpot fits the data better.

We also sought to measure elasticities of demand with respect to effective price to test if revenue-maximising game designs have been chosen for each game. Prices were found to be inelastic for one of the games considered, indicating that this game's effective price is 'too low' from the (narrow) perspective of maximising operator profit.

The composition of the betting coupons (that is, the included teams), was found to have a significant impact on participation (that is, sales). This has to do with the active role of bettors using their knowledge of football teams when making their bets. The usefulness of this marketing tool should be considered by operators.

Finally, according to the different effect of covariates on sales of each game, we can conclude that *La Quiniela* and *El Quinigol* are each catching a different profile of Spanish sport bettor: those who prefer to bet on the final result of several football matches looking for a high jackpot, or those who are attracted to a more difficult game and who are trying to make their bet profitable.

NOTES

1. However, several bookmakers were awarded the first licences to operate sports betting in both the Basque Country and Madrid at the beginning of 2008, opening up a completely new sports betting market. Other legal forms of sport betting in Spain include horse and dog racetrack betting, and gambling on the Basque ball game jai-alai.
2. This also happened in the case of British football pools (Forrest, 1999).
3. In 2006, *La Quiniela* turnover (that is, total sales) was over €480 m, or about €10.89 per inhabitant.
4. Each form can be used to make multiple forecasts, but this may be complicated and is expensive. Moreover, it is usual to form large groups of bettors (*peñas*) to bet on football pools as a way to share the exceptionally high cost of a 'multiple bet'.
5. It must be noted that the LAE only offered this game in 1998 during the Football World Cup and the UEFA Champions League. The game was introduced again in 2000 to coincide with the UEFA European Football Championship and was permanently introduced in 2005; it is now used to bet on matches from the Spanish First Division League (*Liga* BBVA).
6. In 2007, approximately €56 million went to the LFP, so Spanish professional football teams benefit considerably from the pool's funding.
7. We exclude 11, 12 and 13 correct guesses because in those cases, the probability of having at least one winner is almost one.

8. As a sample period, we just consider seasons for which both games were simultaneously available.
9. As the advertised rollover grows, the number of ticket buyers increases as well. The increased number of tickets sold increases the probability of sharing the prize. Thus, the increase in expected return due to rollovers is reduced by the increased number of expected winners, dominating the first effect.
10. Occasionally there are breaks in the Spanish First Division season, so teams in this division are not included in the coupon. The list of games is then composed of Second Division and Second Division B games, National Teams or even teams from other European leagues such as the *Calcio* or *Bundesliga*. In addition, the LAE has also introduced some specific fixtures in the pools referring to European Champions League or other international competitions. It should be noted that the information that Spanish bettors have on these teams is poorer than their knowledge of Spanish teams, so they are likely to be less interested in betting on such fixtures.
11. Football pools in Spain are only offered during the Spanish football season (from the end of August to the following June), unlike in the UK, where Australian games are included in football pools in summer.
12. Given the functional form chosen for the demand equation, the estimated coefficient of the economic variables in logs could be interpreted as short-run elasticities. Long-run elasticities are calculated by dividing these coefficients by one and subtracting the lagged coefficient of the dependent variable.
13. A similar event occurs when Second Division team games are not included on the *La Quiniela* coupon.

REFERENCES

Cook, P. and Clotfelter, C. (1993), 'The Peculiar Scale Economies of Lotto', *American Economic Review*, 83, 634–43.

Farrell, L., Morgenroth, E. and Walker, I. (1999), 'A Time Series Analysis of U.K. Lottery Sales: Long and Short Run Price Elasticities', *Oxford Bulletin of Economics and Statistics*, 61, 513–26.

Farrell, L. and Walker, I. (1999), 'The Welfare Effects of Lotto: Evidence from the UK', *Journal of Public Economics*, 72, 99–120.

Forrest, D. (1999), 'The Past and Future of British Football Pools', *Journal of Gambling Studies*, 15, 161–76.

Forrest, D., Gulley, O. and Simmons, R. (2000), 'Elasticity of Demand for U.K. National Lottery Tickets', *National Tax Journal*, 53, 853–63.

Forrest, D., Simmons, R. and Chesters, N. (2002), 'Buying a Dream: Alternative Models of Demand for Lotto', *Economic Inquiry*, 40, 485–96.

García, J., Pérez, L. and Rodríguez, P. (2008), 'Football Pools Sales: How Important is a Football Club in the Top Divisions?', *International Journal of Sport Finance*, 3, 167–76.

García, J. and Rodríguez, P. (2007), 'The Demand for Football Pools in Spain: The Role of Price, Prizes, and the Composition of the Coupon', *Journal of Sports Economics*, 10, 1–20.

Gulley, O. and Scott, F. (1993), 'The Demand for Wagering on State-Operated Lotto Games', *National Tax Journal*, 46, 13–22.

Scott, F. and Gulley, O. (1995), 'Testing for Efficiency in Lotto Markets', *Economic Inquiry*, 33, 175–88.

Walker, I. (1998), 'The Economic Analysis of Lotteries', *Economic Policy*, 13, 359–92.

8. Is European football's future to become a boring game?

Wladimir Andreff and Gaël Raballand

INTRODUCTION

In recent years, the proportion of matches ending in a 0–0 draw or a 1–0 win has increased in the five major European football leagues. This increase is most pronounced in the more balanced French league. No- or low-scoring games are of concern if we assume that fans prefer watching matches when more goals are scored. Low goal scoring may lead to lower attendances. If the probability of low goal scoring were to grow in future, might it transform European football leagues into boring sporting events? Might it contribute to a drop in attendances? The next logical, follow-on question is to ask what the main factors or drivers are which contribute to no- or low-scoring games. One explanation would simply be the increased adoption of more defensive playing tactics by teams, a factor which might be exacerbated when a game's outcome is of greater significance, that is, a match whose outcome may determine a team's promotion or relegation, given the strong impact of promotion and relegation on future club revenues. Low scoring and defensive tactics may also be triggered by the respective number of points allocated for a win, draw or loss, or by some other football accounting rule to determine the final league standing (goal difference, best defence or best attack criterion).[1] Point allocation may act as a strong incentive structure for a club's strategy.

On the other hand, some major drivers of low goal scoring may be viewed from the vantage point of the league and not the individual club. Thus a further question arises: is there any relationship between a specific league's competitive balance and the percentage of 0–0 and 1–0 scores it generates? Answering this question is important since a linear positive relationship between better competitive balance and bigger league attendance is usually assumed, which may be disturbed if fan interest decreases due to too many low scoring games. The sports economics literature has neither investigated the impact of low goal scoring on fan attendance, nor explored the links between low scores and a league's competitive balance. This chapter looks at this new topic in sports economics.

The chapter is organized as follows: (1) the literature on competitive balance and game attendance is largely silent about goal scoring and its impact on competition and fan attendance; (2) we then present theoretically how 0–0 draws and evenly distributed 1–0 wins must have a significant downward impact on the standard deviation index which is used to assess competitive balance; (3) we demonstrate how over the past century, a long-term tendency towards increasingly defensive tactics has resulted in an overall decrease in the average number of goals scored per game, a major and significant outcome; (4) we then show how a new FIFA rule (three points per win) attempted to reverse this trend, but with little success; (5) we present empirical evidence about the relationship between low goal scoring and competitive balance in major European football leagues both at league level and at club level; (6) a few avenues for further research are briefly sketched; and (7) the chapter concludes by stressing the crucial trade-off between league competitive balance and goal scoring attractiveness, and issues a plea for more goal scoring incentive rules to be instituted.

THE ABSENCE OF GOAL SCORING IN THE COMPETITIVE BALANCE AND GAME ATTENDANCE LITERATURE

Let us imagine a football (soccer) league organised in such a way that all teams have exactly the same probability of winning. The league would enjoy a nearly perfect competitive balance. Now assume that the rules of the game not only allow for games to be drawn but also reward them sufficiently (in terms of points) that draws are considered favourable outcomes when playing very good opponents in professional football. Then, if all teams' sporting strengths were exactly even and equally matched, the most probable league result would be all games emerging as draws. This would be an even more perfect competitive balance. If, by chance, some factor drove teams to systematically adopt defensive tactics on the pitch in such a well-balanced league, then the most probable outcome would be for all games to end in a 0–0 score. The question with such a still more perfect competitive balance (something like a theoretically optimal solution?) is whether stadium attendances and TV audiences would drop because fans might be disappointed with absolutely no goals scored. Too much of competitive balance may kill the uncertainty of outcomes and the expectation of goal scoring, exactly what competitive football is all about.

In major North American professional team sports, the rules for the game are designed to avoid – or at least not facilitate – a tied game. In European football, knockout contests such as Cup tournaments also have competitive rules designed for producing the result of one winner per game. These rules include an additional 30 minutes of extra time play if a 90-minute game ends tied and finally, if a draw remains after extra time, a penalty shootout. The reality of European football leagues, however, is still far from the extreme 'optimal' solution above, particularly when deep financial revenue disparities amongst teams in the same league continue to occur. On the other hand, in European football leagues, a draw is typically rewarded with one point as opposed to three points for a win and zero points for a loss. Therefore, limiting the number of 0–0 outcomes cannot entirely be avoided because of: a) limited competitive effort displayed by one or both teams; b) defensive tactics adopted by one or both teams; and/or c) equal sporting or competitive strengths of the two opposing teams (that is, too much competitive balance).

Goal scoring (or lack of it) has not really been critically explored in the literature surrounding the relationship between competitive balance and game attendance. Neale (1964) opened up the Pandora's box of equating the uncertainty of outcome – the unpredictability of game outcome – with fan attendance. Any league striving for profitability must be adequately balanced to attract substantial crowds. Competitive balance is understood as a positive externality resulting from joint production between teams. In a first standard Walrasian economic model for a professional team sports league, comprised of wage taking and profit maximising teams, El Hodiri and Quirk (1971) introduced the following variables: team revenues, team costs, market size, demand for talent and win percentage. There was no discussion, however, of how wins are achieved – specifically in terms of goal scoring.

Step by step, the standard model has been augmented by the introduction of variables representing specific rules enforced in North American professional leagues: a reserve clause, a rookie draft, a salary cap, revenue redistribution between teams, rent sharing between players and team owners (Fort and Quirk, 1995; Scully, 1995; Késenne, 2000a), and others. However, despite variations in the standard model, one cannot find anything specifically addressing the impact of goal scoring on league economic equilibrium and sporting competitive balance. A good excuse exists for this omission: the reference is commonly a North American closed league where presumably goal scoring has much less significance in comparison to an open league, since team standings and relegation/promotion outcomes are not decided on goal difference between teams in North American professional sports leagues.

When it comes to analysing European football open leagues with the standard model, Sloane (1971) assumed that clubs are win maximising instead of profit maximising. Adapting the model to such a club's objective function has not changed the assortment of variables which need to be taken into consideration (Késenne, 1996, 2000b). Since 2003, the theory of team professional sports leagues has been amended after giving up the assumption of a fixed supply of talent. This has occurred because national leagues face a flexible supply in a post-Bosman global market for talent with labour mobility from league to league (both between countries and between lower and upper leagues). With a flexible supply of talent, the standard Walrasian model of competitive balance no longer holds; it must be replaced by a Nash-equilibrium model of a non-cooperative game (Szymanski, 2003, 2004; Szymanski and Késenne, 2004). As a better fit with European football open leagues (Andreff, 2009), the new model still relies on the same variables as the Walrasian standard, and goal scoring remains an unexplored variable.

From a fan's point of view, the quality of games (contests) may be as important as a home team's win. As well as identification with a team, fan interest is stimulated by demonstration of the physical or mental capabilities of a team, which often depend on which players have been selected in the squad (superstars, 'local heroes', veterans, rookies). In addition, fans are attracted by the 'level of drama', which depends on the degree of contention and uncertainty of outcome, all variables encompassed in the quality of a game. Notice that the number of goals scored does not show up as a quality dimension of a game in the survey by Borland and Macdonald (2003).

Since the literature on game attendance maintains a link between the uncertainty of outcome and competitive balance, all the variables used in the model of professional team leagues can enter by the back door. However, econometric testing provides a blurred message: seven studies of football, rugby and cricket attendance have exhibited a positive and significant relationship between the uncertainty of outcome and game attendance, while three studies exclusively devoted to English football have raised doubts about the relevance of such a relationship (Peel and Thomas, 1992; Baimbridge *et al.*, 1996; Forrest and Simmons, 2002).

Additional variables appear among the determinants of game attendance: price of admission and fans' income (Andreff, 1981; Bird, 1982; Simmons, 1996); travel costs (Forrest *et al.*, 2002); availability of substitutes such as TV terrestrial and satellite broadcasts (Baimbridge *et al.*, 1996); competing sporting events; the club's age; the proportion of manual workers in the town (Dobson and Goddard, 1995); promotion and relegation (Simmons, 1996); quality of viewing – quality of seating, stadium size, parking availability, timing of contest (Andreff and Nys, 1986; McDonald and Rascher, 2000); home field advantage (Forrest and Simmons, 2002); supply capacity; and macroeconomic variables such as the rate of unemployment in the club's market area. The quality of a game and its impact on attendance are also linked to sporting determinants such as recent performance of the home club, its current league position, points scored in previous home games, and ranking of the opposing team (Cairns, 1987). Though Cairns' article mentions *point* scoring as an attendance determinant, it does not pay attention to *goal* scoring.

Another factor relevant to game attendance was found to be the degree of game contention (Jennett, 1984; Borland, 1987; Cairns, 1987; Dobson and Goddard, 1992), which is often higher by the end of a game than by half time. It is not comparable at the beginning and close to the end of season. It depends on whether a team's standing is either high enough for promotion (or Champions League qualification) or low enough to risk being relegated, and on how many games remain before the end of the season. The degree of contention is one interesting variable found in our literature review since it has a high probability of influencing goal scoring strategies when teams are ranked according to wins and draws and, at the end of the day, by goal difference. However, just one econometric testing of a demand function for English football attendance has encompassed goal scoring as an explanatory variable (Simmons, 1996). Scoring showed up as statistically significant for nine out of nineteen sampled teams. Simmons found that casual spectators are more influenced by goal scoring than are season ticket holders. This interesting result has not led to further research so far. Thus the existing literature is nearly an empty shell with regard to our variable of interest: goal scoring has not been paid much attention by sports economists, in the case of European football.

The uncertainty of outcome is to be considered when it is understood as a relationship between the degrees of competitive balance on the one hand and fan interest and financial health of a professional sport league on the other hand. The trick in this approach is that increasing revenue inequality between teams tends to reduce league competitive balance (makes it more unbalanced) and subsequently a decreasing degree of competitive balance tends to reduce fan interest and game attendance (Jennett, 1984). Financial disparities between clubs have increased substantially in major European football leagues in the past ten years or so (Andreff, 2009). Those teams playing in both national and European (Champions League, UEFA Cup) contests have a much larger stream of revenues and, as a consequence, a much larger budget to attract talent, than teams which perform only at national level; the former qualify again and again for European contests and benefit from a financial virtuous circle whereas the latter are locked in a vicious circle of lower revenue and weaker sporting results. Thus, increasing inequality in revenues between teams is a strong driver for competitive balance decline with a negative impact on fan attendance. Szymanski (2001) found that increasing inter-division financial inequality among participant teams in the FA Cup between 1976 and 1998 led to a decline in fan attendance. Various studies have exhibited a significant relationship between financial inequalities across teams and low (unbalanced) competitive balance (Szymanski and Kuypers, 1999; Andreff and Bourg, 2006; Gerrard, 2006). When Granger causality is tested, clubs' revenues (Davies *et al.*, 1995) and wages (Hall *et al.*, 2002) are determinants of sporting results and team standings, that is, the balance of sporting contest.

SCORING AND COMPETITIVE BALANCE

A recent work has underlined a trend towards more competitive imbalance in the English League in the long run and its possible negative implications for fans (Groot, 2008). Groot starts with the usual (so-called Noll-Scully) index, defined as the standard deviation in win percentages compared with the average win percentage:

$$S = \sigma / (0{,}5 / \sqrt{N}), \text{ with: } \sigma = \sqrt{\Sigma_i (v_i - 0.5)^2} \qquad (8.1)$$

With such a measure, in a perfectly balanced league, each team has a win percentage v_i equal to 0.5, then S equals zero and competitive balance reaches its maximum. The more scattered the win percentages are throughout all teams, the higher the standard deviation, and the lower the degree of competitive balance; in a perfectly unbalanced league, this degree would decline toward zero. This pertains to static competitive balance. Groot also measures dynamic competitive balance with a Kendall's rank correlation coefficient between team standings in one season and their standing in adjacent seasons. Then he introduces goal scoring as a Poisson process. Let Y represent the number of goals scored in a game by a team, which can take on the values 0, 1, 2, 3. . ., then:

$$P(Y = y) = e^{-\mu} \mu^y / y! \qquad (8.2)$$

The single parameter of the Poisson distribution μ reflects the propensity to score goals. The Poisson process of goal scoring allows the expected win probabilities to be calculated for any team. This calculation enables a derivation of the expected average number of goals scored per game, the expected average number of goals allowed per game, and the expected goal difference d ($d = 0$ is the probability of a draw). With such statistical calculation, goal scoring is linked to win percentages and, by the same token, to competitive balance indexes.[2]

The aforementioned methodology applied to English football over 107 seasons between 1888–2006 exhibits a tendency of both static and dynamic competitive balances to decline in the long run, that is, to move towards a more unbalanced league, whether measured with traditional or new competitive balance indexes. On the other hand, over the past century, the average number of goals per game has significantly decreased, which has had a beneficial upward effect on competitive balance. Without this fall in scoring, the decline in competitive balance would have been sharper. Groot suggests that, because team qualities widened, teams of lesser standing have relied on defensive strategies to minimise the number of goals allowed per game in order to raise their chance of drawing or winning against higher ranked teams. If this is so, the decline in competitive balance is the cause and the decline in average scoring the effect. Whatever the causality, both variables are tightly linked.

Competitive balance decline has accelerated since the start of the Champions League in its present form in 1994–95. The process of growing league imbalance goes slowly, but unmistakably, in the same direction. According to Groot, competitive balance decline has reached a frightening pace in the last decade: 'success in one season breeds success in the following season, and that failure breeds failure'. Shorter time series are provided to back the same conclusion in other major European football leagues: Italy, France, Germany, Spain and the Netherlands.

In the English Premier League, the first factor influencing the level of competitive balance is the average number of goals per game:[3] the lower the average number of goals, the higher the level of competitive balance. And vice versa: the higher the average number of goals per game, the more unbalanced the league. In European football, uncertainty of outcome has become more of a myth than a reality in the past decade.

In line with Groot's analysis, we derive that 0–0 scores definitely lower the average number of goals per match and 1–0 scores lower it relative to any other score except 0–0. Thus, low goal scoring must be correlated with a higher level of competitive balance. More precisely, a 0–0 draw is more pro-competitive balance than any other drawn game for two reasons: it absolutely lowers the average number of goals in the league and does not affect any secondary ranking criteria such as best attack and best defence (and of course goal difference). A 1–0 win is more pro-competitive balance than any other win for two reasons as well: it lowers the average number of goals in the league and has less effect on secondary ranking criteria (goal difference, best attack and/or best defence) than any other winning score. Our expectation is that more balanced European football leagues have a higher proportion of 0–0 and 1–0 scores than more unbalanced leagues.

Groot infers a policy implication from his analysis which runs against a European Superleague such as the one supported by Hoehn and Szymanski (1999). It is coined 'back to the 1950s' and amounts to a rejection of the present Media-Corporation-Merchandising-Market (MCMM) model of sport finance, where the great bulk of club revenues stems from TV broadcasting rights (Andreff and Staudohar, 2000), while returning to the former Spectators-Subsidies-Sponsors model based on gate receipts. This would be likely to stop the decline in competitive balance. Groot admits that his solution to restore a higher level of competitive balance is radical and naïve since it implies less TV money poured into football with free-to-air broadcast of integral football games and highlights for free. A professional football league can hardly accept such a solution given the current dependence on TV broadcasting rights revenues. Groot fails to point out that his solution also incurs a decline in average goal scoring, which means an increase in 1–0 and 0–0 scores. How can one avoid the increased attractiveness due to higher competitive balance being offset by a boring effect of no (few) goal scored?

The Champions League new format and the Bosman case co-incided in 1995 and impacted on competitive balance in European leagues. Table 8.1 confirms a slight decline in static competitive balance over the subsequent twelve years in the five major European football leagues, since the Noll-Scully index is increasing on average in four leagues, while in the French *Ligue 1*, the index even fell below 1 in 1999–2000. From 1996–97 to 2007–08, after French *Ligue 1*, the most balanced leagues were the Spanish *Liga de Futbol* and the German *Bundesliga*. The Italian *Lega Calcio* and English Premier League were the least balanced. One expectation to be verified is that the number of low scoring games must be higher in France. A correlation is expected to show up between competitive balance indexes and goal scoring indicators.

Similar expectations can be derived from Table 8.2, with a dynamic competitive balance calculated as a (here Spearman not Kendall) rank correlation between club standing in one season and the next season. The French *Ligue 1* exhibits by far the highest level of dynamic competitive balance. In 2000–01, the French league was balanced with a rank correlation equal to zero. The next season's outcome was absolutely unpredictable. With this index, the German *Bundesliga* is the second-best balanced contest while the Spanish *Liga de Futbol* joins the Italian *Calcio* and the English Premier League among the lowest degrees of competitive balance.

Table 8.1   *Competitive balance in five European football leagues after 1995*

Season	Ligue 1 France	Premier League England	Lega Calcio Italy	Liga de Futbol Spain	Bundesliga Germany
1996/97	1.47	1.23	1.33	1.61	1.43
1997/98	1.31	1.28	1.76	1.39	1.14
1998/99	1.42	1.52	1.35	1.41	1.52
1999/2000	0.88	1.69	1.65	1.03	1.43
2000/01	1.15	1.43	1.60	1.29	1.14
2001/02	1.18	1.72	1.71	1.14	1.54
2002/03	1.28	1.62	1.56	1.32	1.23
2003/04	1.46	1.57	1.86	1.28	1.61
2004/05	1.10	1.73	1.45	1.51	1.50
2005/06	1.44	1.94	1.97	1.49	1.53
2006/07	1.06	1.64	1.78	1.39	1.30
2007/08	1.36	2.09	1.60	1.46	1.47
Mean	**1.26**	**1.62**	**1.64**	**1.36**	**1.40**

Note: This table is based on the Noll-Scully index.

Source: Andreff (2009).

Competitive balance, though a useful concept, does not tell the whole story about why fans are attracted to stadiums or to watch matches on TV. When tied games are allowed, as in football, it must be assumed that the greater the number of draws, the better the competitive balance. A better competitive balance should then trigger bigger attendances. Imagine one league with only 0–0 tied games and another with only 3–3 draws in all games. Competitive balance would be the same, but fans would probably be bored with the former, preferring many goals in the latter. Or compare two leagues with exactly the same competitive balance but where in one all games are won 1–0 while in the other all games are won 3–2; it is obvious which league fans would prefer to attend. The number of goals scored matters for game and league attendance.

One of Forrest and Simmons's (2002, our italics) conclusions is that 'although soccer fans appear to prefer well-balanced games, given absolute performance levels of competing teams, the impos- ition of equality of strength across clubs would nevertheless run the

Table 8.2 Dynamic competitive balance in five European football leagues after 1995

Season	*Ligue 1* France	Premier League England	*Lega Calcio* Italy	*Liga de Futbol* Spain	*Bundesliga* Germany
1996/97	0.50	0.63	n.a.	0.55	0.34
1997/98	0.46	0.43	0.65	0.61	0.39
1998/99	0.49	0.71	0.53	0.71	0.37
1999/2000	0.24	0.83	0.81	0.59	0.70
2000/01	**0.00**	0.88	0.85	0.65	0.25
2001/02	0.08	0.61	0.75	0.61	0.69
2002/03	0.28	0.63	0.62	0.55	0.53
2003/04	0.60	0.43	0.81	0.45	0.44
2004/05	0.68	0.45	0.64	0.59	0.61
2005/06	0.67	0.66	0.43	0.48	0.75
2006/07	0.48	0.66	0.52	0.58	0.72
2007/08	0.20	0.66	0.65	0.59	0.49

Note: This table based on the rank correlation between clubs standing in t and $t - 1$ seasons.

Source: Andreff (2009).

risk of lowering attendances'. A comparable risk must be envisaged with goal scoring: although fans prefer well-balanced games, 0–0 and 1–0 scores that reflect evenness or closeness of strength run the risk of lowering attendances. With its best competitive balance, French *Ligue 1* is at most risk.

RISING DEFENSIVE TACTICS ON THE FOOTBALL PITCH: AN HISTORICAL TREND

A French sociologist (Avrillier, 1978) was one of the first to notice that, in the long run, an increasing inflow of money into football was fuelling a tendency for teams to move to increasingly defensive tactics on the pitch. When big revenues are at stake, losing a match is more costly than winning it is beneficial, both from sporting and economic perspectives. Losses increase the risk of relegation or missing promotion, dissuade fans from attending and increase the financial risk for the club – both in the current and the next season in the case of relegation. Wins are not always beneficial, namely when a team is not in contention for promotion or relegation in the second half of the season. In such circumstances, wins do not attract big attendances and gate revenues, while the club budget has usually been built on the assumption of winning more than losing, but this does not compare with the financial shock of relegation. The more money at stake in being relegated or not promoted, the more costly is the loss. Avrillier contended that changing tactics on the pitch from WM (see below) to 4–2–4 then 4–3–3 was teams' reaction to the increased cost of a defeat.

With increasing revenues at stake, the number of teams and games in contention increases. Then, the higher the contention, the higher the significance of match outcome for a team, and the more defensive tactics are adopted. Since the number of goals partly depends on scoring tactics adopted by each team on the pitch, a realistic assumption is that a team's tactics are not independent of the club's objective function. Is this win maximising, as usually assumed in European football leagues? If such an assumption is made, then the following puzzle emerges: why win-maximising teams behave in such a way that the number of 0–0 and 1–0 outcomes is increasing. Increasingly, defensive tactics do not fit with a win-maximising objective, but with a strategy which emphasises not losing. Such a strategy translates on the pitch into many teams pursuing a loss-minimising rather than a win-maximising objective.

Raballand *et al.* (2008) observed an increase of 0–0 scores in major European football leagues, indicating a historical trend towards defensive tactics. When the first rules of the game were adopted by the new Football Association in 1863 in England, it was common to witness very offensive tactics, with no more than the goalkeeper and one or two other players in defence. Games were high scoring. In 1867, an offside rule was adopted, stating that a forward player was not offside as long as at least three opponents (the goalkeeper and two others) were standing between him and the goal line. Then more sophisticated tactics based on repeatedly passing the ball across forward players developed. On the other hand, defenders rapidly found how they could use the offside rule to break up opponents' attacks. Defences started prevailing over attacks and the number of free kicks for offside swiftly increased. In 1925, the number of defenders between the forward and the goal line was reduced to two and the number of goals scored immediately grew by 30 per cent, while the number of free kicks for offside decreased. The same year Arsenal invented the so-called WM tactics with five forwards, two midfielders, and three defenders.

The tactics evolved throughout the 20th century, always in the same direction: more and more defensive. In the 1950s, 4–2–4 tactics (four defenders, two midfielders and four forwards) spreading enabled Brazil to win the 1958 World Cup. At the 1962 World Cup, Brazil adopted a more defensive 4–3–3 tactic and won with only three forwards. In Italy, teams developed the famous *catenacio* ('bolt'), concentrating no less than seven players in defence. The number of goals dropped markedly in the *Lega Calcio*. Since the 1990s, most teams have played 4–4–2 or 4–5–1, leaving just one or two forwards facing four defenders, whose number may instantaneously become eight or nine. The consequence of 4–4–2 and 4–5–1 is that almost the whole team falls back in defence as soon as they have lost the ball, so that for much of the game, most players are concentrated in the middle of the pitch. On the other hand, when a team is dominating, nearly all players of both teams are grouped in and around one penalty area. The game has become rather standardised and stereotyped. When most players are struggling in midfield and defence, just one or two isolated forward(s) have a very low probability of scoring except on the counter-attack, or from corners or free kicks. The defence nearly always prevails over the attack of a defensive team. Such tactics have the objective of maintaining a leading or a tied score rather than trying to score again.

With widespread defensive tactics, there are few other possible outcomes than low goal scoring in many games, and a decreasing trend in the average number of goals per game. The trend is clear: the average number of goals scored in the English league fell from 4.44 in 1889 to 2.48 in 2006, from about 4.3 in 1929 to 2.2 in 1989 in the *Liga de Futbol*, from 4.51 in 1934 to 2.13 in 2006 in *Ligue 1*, and from 3.57 in 1964 to 2.81 in the *Bundesliga*, whereas it has nearly always been below 3.0 in *Lega Calcio* since 1930 (see Appendix A).

Starting from the above historical observations about defensive tactics, Raballand *et al.* (2008) contend that football games are becoming increasingly boring. Many match outcomes directly depend on refereeing decisions and defence fouls. It is increasingly difficult to score without penalty kicks, corners or free kicks: a high proportion of goals is scored right after a refereeing decision such as a penalty kick, free kick or corner – 30 per cent of all goals in French *Ligue 1*, in 2006–07.[4] Then, once it has scored, a team adopts defensive tactics to prevent any further goal. As a result, the average number of goals per match has decreased in major European football leagues. The football show is less enjoyable than some decades ago. For instance, French fans are frustrated that more than one-third of *Ligue 1* games end up with at best one goal scored. A number of teams systematically adopt from the beginning of each game tactics geared towards not conceding goals. Clearly, if both teams adopt such tactics, the game is destined for a 0–0 draw. This is always better than a defeat when promotion or relegation is at stake, whatever the quality of the show.

It is striking that the trend towards low goal scoring has coincided, since 1995–96, with the skyrocketing growth in TV rights revenues that is associated with the MCMM model of sport finance[5] and the increasing gap between the budgets of the richest and poorest clubs. In English Premier League, the budget gap between the richest and poorest clubs widened: from 1 to 4 in 1994 up to 1 to 8 in 2003. Moreover, revenue concentration goes along with win concentration (Andreff, 2009; Andreff and Bourg, 2006). In 2008, Manchester United, Chelsea, Arsenal and Liverpool were the first four clubs ranked in the Premier League for the third year in a row; they were the richest as well. Despite the higher competitive balance in French *Ligue 1*, Olympique Lyonnais won the championship seven years in a row from 2001–02 to 2007–08. Although a loss is a normal and regular outcome of a game, Raballand *et al.* contend that a loss is increasingly incompatible with growing TV rights revenues invested in a team. Such investment is achieved only if the risk of economic loss is limited, which implies minimising the risk of losing on the pitch. More money in football translates into more defensive tactics to avoid losing. Only the richest clubs able to pay for the most talented players can afford non-defensive tactics in high contention games – and they often win them.

Recommendations put forward by Raballand *et al.* (2008) to improve the attractiveness of games and alleviate the boring aspect of low goal scoring include: (a) reduce promotion and relegation to just one club in French *Ligue 1*, so that the number of games that trigger the most defensive tactics will diminish; (b) change the points reward as follows: 3 points for a win, 1 point for a scoring draw, *½ point for a 0–0 draw* and 0 points for a loss, which is assumed to reduce the number of 0–0 tied games; (c) give up the offside rule outside the penalty box; and (d) temporary player exclusion after a foul as in ice hockey and rugby. If such measures succeeded in reducing the number of 0–0 and 1–0 scores, the average number of goals per game would increase, but competitive balance would decline automatically more than observed by Groot, due to revenue inequalities and uneven access to TV revenues.

IS THE DOWNWARD GOAL SCORING TREND EXACERBATED BY FIFA RULES?

To try to reverse the historical trend to more defensive and, from the fans' point of view, less exciting tactics, FIFA changed the rules, increasing the reward for a win from two to three points. Was it a success?

At the same time as the Bosman case and the new Champions League format, in the 1995–96 season, FIFA raised the reward for a win in football games from two to three points. Three main objectives were assigned to this rule change: more goals per game, fewer draws, and on top of this, more exciting and attractive games. A number of papers have tested the new rule impact on the number of draws and scoring with ambiguous results, while a game theory analysis has concluded that the new rule must be counterproductive. Some studies have validated the efficiency of the new rule. Guedes and Machado (2002) have found that in the Portuguese premier league, only weaker teams played significantly more offensively after the rule change, whereas only stronger teams were able to score significantly more goals per game than before the change. Working on former Soviet, Ukrainian and Italian *Serie A* league data, Shepotylo (2006) has shown a substantial decrease in the number of draws but a high incentive for collusion in games between teams of nearly equal strength because the reward for one win plus one loss each (3 points) is higher than the reward for two draws each (2 points). Aylott and Aylott (2007) demonstrated that, with data from seven countries, in six of them the average number of goals per game increased, but the number of draws increased as well. Dilger and Geyer (2009) have demonstrated with German *Bundesliga* data that the three points rule has significantly decreased the number of draws in league games (by comparison with cup games, where the rule does not apply) while the goal difference in games has shrunk. The number of 0–0 draws decreased insignificantly.

Other studies call into question the effectiveness of the three points rule in achieving its three main objectives. Amann, Dewenter and Namini (2004) have shown with German league data that the number of goals and the number of wins significantly declined. Hundsdoerfer (2004) has demonstrated empirically that both the average number of goals and the average number of offensive moves have decreased in the *Bundesliga*. Garicano and Palacios-Huerta (2006) have shown that the number of draws and the number of games with a goal difference of two or more goals has decreased significantly while the number of shots on goal and corner kicks, yellow cards (serious fouls) and games with a goal difference of one has increased. Further inferences derived by Garicano and Palacios-Huerta are a greater incentive to unfair play after the new FIFA rule and decreasing fan interest and game attendance.

One theoretical paper relying on game theory demonstrates a counterproductive effect of the three points rule (Brocas and Carrillo, 2004), going far beyond the contention that the new rule has simply devalued a draw relative to a win from one-half to one-third. The core idea is that optimal tactics on the pitch depend on the current score at any moment. With the three points rule, adopting offensive tactics increases a team's chances of scoring but also of conceding a goal. Then, in the case of a game being drawn (all games start at 0–0), increasing the value of a win will induce a stronger team A to adopt more offensive tactics towards the end of the game in order to break the tie in one direction or another late in the match. The weaker opposing team B will of course play as defensively as possible toward the end of the game and, if successful, will obtain a 0–0 draw. However, it will also induce teams to use more defensive tactics toward the beginning of the game in order to avoid going behind early in the match and therefore keep the option of trying to break the tie late in the match. A leading team is enticed to play as defensively as possible and, if successful, this explains why 1–0 scores are so common. As a result, nearly all teams will play more defensively with three points than two points for a win. The fact that a team can change tactics over the course of the match makes the new rule counterproductive. A tentative conclusion is that the long-run trend in rising defensive tactics on the pitch has seemingly even been strengthened by the three points rule.

COMPETITIVE BALANCE AND GOAL SCORING

Preliminary empirical evidence about the relationship between goal scoring and competitive balance in the five major European football leagues overall is provided in Table 8.3. Tables 8B.3a to 8B.3e (Appendix 8B) show the same data for each national league. Over a short span of time (2002–03 to 2006–07), it is not possible to confirm either the historical trend toward competitive balance decline or a sharp increase in low scoring games. Nevertheless it is witnessed that:

1. The cumulative percentage of 0–0 and 1–0 scores is rather high – together more than a quarter of all scores – and every year is bigger than the number of games with more than four goals.
2. When the Noll-Scully index increases (leagues become less balanced), the percentage of 0–0 and 1–0 scores decreases whereas a standard deviation decrease (more balanced leagues) is associated with an increase in 0–0 and 1–0 scores, in accordance with aforementioned analytical expectations.
3. The percentage of 0–0 scores increases in the five leagues on average.
4. The attractiveness ratio, defined as the ratio between games with more than four goals and games with a maximum of one goal, is stagnant or declining, except in 2004.
5. The ratio between the number of 0–0 scores and the number of games with more than four goals, a sort of disincentive ratio, has evolved as follows: 43.8 per cent in 2003, 37.8 per cent in 2004, 46.9 per cent in 2005, 49.2 per cent in 2006 and 49.5 per cent in 2007, a mostly rising tendency.
6. Overall, the *average number of goals per game has slightly decreased*, except in 2004, which is consistent with the rise in 0–0 and 1–0 scores.

All observations suggest that the future of European football is to become a more boring game. The most worrying are the last four, except if fans are eager to attend more and more games with 0–0 scores and with a decreasing average of goals.

The five major leagues are not all in the same position compared with the overall picture in Table 8.3. The worst case is the French *Ligue 1* (see Table 8B.3a). The cumulative number of 0–0 and 1–0

Table 8.3 Competitive balance and goal scoring, five major European leagues

Season	2003	2004	2005	2006	2007	Average
Competitive balance*	1.40	1.56	1.46	1.67	1.43	1.50
A = % of 0–0 scores/all scores	**8.4**	**8.5**	**9.0**	**9.0**	**10.0**	**9.0**
B = % of 1–0 scores/all scores	20.0	17.6	19.6	18.7	19.3	19.0
C = % of games with max. 1 goal	*28.4*	*26.0*	*28.6*	*27.7*	*29.2*	*28.0*
D = % of games with > 4 goals	19.2	22.5	19.2	18.3	20.2	19.9
E = D/C = attractiveness ratio	0.68	0.87	0.67	0.66	0.69	0.71
Number of goals per game	2.55	2.66	2.55	2.50	2.49	2.55

Note: *Noll-Scully index, 5 league average (from Table 8.1).

Source: Data from *Bundesliga, Lega Calcio, Liga de Futbol, Ligue 1* and Premier League.

scores is more than three times bigger than the number of games with more than four goals. The attractiveness ratio is the lowest (between 0.17 and 0.39). About 13 per cent of games end up with no goal, a percentage much higher than in other leagues. A French fan has one chance out of seven of seeing no goal before the game ends. The disincentive ratio between the number of 0–0 scores and the number of games with more than four goals has evolved from 111.7 per cent in 2003 to 78.5 per cent in 2004, 179.7 per cent in 2005, 97.8 per cent in 2006 and a disastrous 222.4 per cent in 2007. This last year the probability of attending a game with no goal was more than twice that of attending a game with more than four goals. As a result, the French *Ligue 1* has the *lowest* average number of goals per game and is the least appealing league!

The German *Bundesliga* (Table 8B.3b) is the opposite of the French *Ligue 1*. It is fairly balanced but, on average, (1) is not verified, since in three years out of five, the number of games with more than four goals has been bigger than the cumulative number of 0–0 and 1–0 scores. The attractiveness ratio is the highest (between 0.91 and 1.33) among the five leagues. The (2) relationship is not verified either, a German exception. The trend in 0–0 scores is upwards but with the lowest percentage compared to the other four leagues. The disincentive ratio is low, between 22.2 per cent and 37.3 per cent. The probability of a German fan attending a game with more than four goals is three–four times higher than that of attending a game without any goal. Thus, the *Bundesliga* has the highest average number of goals per game.

The Spanish *Liga de Futbol* (Table 8B.3c) is also fairly balanced and (1) is verified. The number of 0–0 scores is fluctuating as the second lowest average after the *Bundesliga*, though one cannot perceive an increasing trend as in Germany. The attractiveness ratio is rather high (between 0.67 and 0.87), but lower than in the *Bundesliga*. The disincentive ratio has fluctuated between 24.5 per cent and 40.3 per cent. The Spanish *Liga de Futbol* is in the middle of the sample as regards its average number of goals per game. All in all, with regard to goal scoring, the *Bundesliga* is an attractive though quite balanced league and the *Liga de Futbol* is about the same, but less attractive with a lower number of goals. On the other hand, the most balanced *Ligue 1* suffers all low goal scoring issues: many 0–0 scores; many scores with no more than one goal; and few games with more than four goals.

The English Premier League (Table 8B.3d) is one of the two most unbalanced leagues. The (2) relationship does not apply very well whereas (1) is absolutely verified. Beyond a peak in 2004, the number of 0–0 scores increases. The attractiveness ratio is on average the lowest (between 0.57 and 0.88) after the French *Ligue 1*. Given high attendances in the Premier League, English fans seem quite ready to face the probability of low scoring. The disincentive ratio is between 27.9 per cent and 49.1 per cent. English fans have a higher probability of attending a game with no goals relative to a more than four goal match than Spanish or German fans. The attractiveness of the Premier League is partly a myth compared to other major leagues apart from the French *Ligue 1*, since it has the second lowest average number of goals per game. On the other hand, league imbalance does not translate into such a high proportion of more than four goal matches, compared with the two more balanced leagues.

The Italian *Lega Calcio* (Table 8B.3e) is the most unbalanced league, but both the (2) and (1) relationships are verified. The number of 0–0 scores is the second highest but fluctuates more than really increasing. The disincentive ratio is between 35.7 per cent and 53.1 per cent. The attractiveness ratio is similar to the Spanish one, but with a wider dispersion (between 0.56 and 1.17). League imbalance does not translate into either much fewer 0–0 results or a higher proportion of games with more than four goals (nearly at the same level as the Spanish league). Contrary to preconceived ideas linked to the *catenacio* reputation, the *Lega Calcio* is the league with the second highest average number of goals per game, after the *Bundesliga*.

Those characteristics exhibited at the level of the five leagues together roughly fit with each national league except for the *Bundesliga*. The French *Ligue 1* is the best example of the expected relationship between high competitive balance, low goal scoring and the rise in 0–0 and 1–0 scores. On the other hand, we did not find that more balanced leagues (except *Ligue 1*) have more 0–0 results, which are more numerous in the unbalanced Italian and English leagues than in the Spanish and German leagues. Looking for a clue to this puzzling observation requires a club-level analysis (beyond the scope of this chapter) to check whether defensive tactics are correlated with more uneven club revenue concentration in Italy and England.

At club level, our data panel gathered 486 observations: 20 teams × 5 years = 100 teams each in the Premier League, *Liga de Futbol* and *Ligue 1*, 18 teams × 5 years = 90 teams in the *Bundesliga*, and 18 teams × 2 years + 20 teams × 3 years = 96 teams in the *Lega Calcio*, where the number of clubs in *Serie A* increased from 18 in 2004 to 20 in 2005.

We test whether the team standings at the end of the season, the dispersion of which is competitive balance, are determined by goal scoring. The standing variable is PTS_i, the number of points per team i at the end of the season. Goal scoring variables are: GF_i, goals for, which measures the attacking quality of team i, GA_i, goals conceded, which measures how defensive a team is, $(0\text{–}0\ Scores)_i$, the percentage of no-goal scores achieved by team i, $(1\text{–}0\ Scores)_i$, the percentage of 1–0 scores[6] achieved by team i, a $LEAGUE_{ji}$ dummy depending on which European league j team i belongs to, with the French *Ligue 1* as the reference, and a $YEAR_{ik}$ dummy with 2003 as the reference,[7] in equation (8.3):

$$PTS_i = k + aGF_i + bGA_i + c(0-0\,Scores)_i + d(1-0\,Scores)_i$$

$$+ \sum_j e_j LEAGUE_{ji} + \sum_k f_k YEAR_{ki} + \varepsilon_i \qquad (8.3)$$

Goals for is a significant variable in explaining a team's standing and the coefficient is positive (Table 8.4): the better a team's attack, the better its standing, which is trivial. If a leading team wants to qualify for the Champions League, it must have strong forwards. If an underdog wants to escape relegation, its forwards must not be too inefficient in scoring. Goals conceded is also significant, but with a negative sign: the lower number of goals allowed, that is, the better a team's defence, the better its standing. A prevailing team which aims at Champions League qualification must have one of the best defences in the league and therefore defensive tactics that operate efficiently. Relegated underdogs are those with insufficiently efficient defence tactics. It follows that, whether contending for promotion or relegation, a team will adopt the most defensive tactics available to it.

The percentage of 0–0 results is significant at a 5 per cent threshold with a negative coefficient. A team which has too many 0–0 draws cannot aspire to promotion (or Champions League qualification); it does not play for the final victory. Teams with the greatest number of 0–0 draws are not those in contention for promotion; they are to be found among those in danger of relegation (roughly the bottom

Table 8.4 *The relationship between clubs' standings and goal scoring*

Dependent variable: points (standing)	PTS	Model 1: OLS			Model 2: Random effects		
		Coefficient	Robust standard error	P > |t|	Coefficient	Standard error	P > |t|
Goals for (best attack)	GF	0.7395	0.0261	0.000***	0.7405	0.0264	0.000***
Goals allowed (best defence)	GA	−0.6202	0.0277	0.000***	−0.6179	0.0281	0.000***
% of 0–0 scores	(0–0 Scores)	−10.4474	5.1239	0.042**	−10.1144	5.3386	0.058*
% of 1–0 scores	(1–0 Scores)	10.5204	3.8737	0.007***	10.6455	3.7166	0.004***
Germany dummy	LEAGUE 2	−5.1307	0.7195	0.000***	−5.1199	0.7624	0.000***
England dummy	LEAGUE 3	−0.0578	0.6311	0.927	−0.0629	0.6602	0.924
Italy dummy	LEAGUE 4	−2.9058	0.6481	0.000***	−2.9200	0.6513	0.000***
Spain dummy	LEAGUE 5	−0.3049	0.6202	0.623	−0.3096	0.6652	0.642
2004 dummy	YEAR 1	0.0074	0.6008	0.990	0.0036	0.6029	0.995
2005 dummy	YEAR 2	0.6809	0.5575	0.223	0.6782	0.5991	0.258
2006 dummy	YEAR 3	1.1491	0.5946	0.054*	1.1563	0.5975	0.053*
2007 dummy	YEAR 4	0.7846	0.6511	0.229	0.7735	0.6417	0.228
Constant	k	44.6695	3.1119	0.000***	44.4525	3.2185	0.000***
		Number of obs = 486			Number of obs = 486		
		$F_{(12, 455)} = 326.34$			Wald chi2 (12) = 4816.17		
		Prob > F = 0.0000			Prob > chi2 = 0.0000		
		R2 = 0.9174			R2 = 0.9174		
		Root MSE = 4.1844			Breusch Pagan: Prob > chi2 = 0.8482		

Notes: * Significant at a 10% threshold; ** at a 5% threshold; *** at a 1% threshold.

Source: Data from *Bundesliga, Lega Calcio, Liga de Futbol, Ligue 1* and Premier League.

half of the league table) in which defensive tactics are essential during the second half of the season. The percentage of 1–0 scores is significant at 1 per cent, with a positive coefficient. The greater the number of 1–0 wins, as for any winning score, the better the standing. A number of games with a high degree of competition produce a 1–0 result. When a leading team plays another leading team, either team will be satisfied with a 1–0 win, and will adopt the game strategy presented by Brocas and Carrillo (2004). Underdogs often aim at winning 1–0 when playing against any team; this consists in adopting defensive tactics to earn a 0–0 draw at worst and, with luck, just score once on a counter-attack or from a free kick and then 'close the door'.

Looking at the *LEAGUE* dummy, it is significant with a negative coefficient for Germany and Italy. Since the French *Ligue 1* is the reference league, to reach the same position, a German *Bundesliga* (Italian *Lega Calcio*) team scores more goals, allows fewer goals, and achieves fewer 0–0 scores and more 1–0 scores than a French team. The English Premier League and the Spanish *Liga de Futbol* are not significantly different from *Ligue 1*, which means that goal scoring and defensive tactics are not much different in these three leagues. This result is consistent with the previous empirical observation that *Ligue 1*, Premier League and *Liga de Futbol* are those leagues with the lowest average numbers of goals per game (Tables 8B.3a–e). Finally, year dummy variables are not significant, except 2006 (at a 10 per cent threshold), which means that the results are not significantly different from those of the reference year 2003. The 2006 exception is probably due to the exceptional degree of competitive imbalance (Table 8.1) reached in the Premier League (1.94) and even more so in *Lega Calcio* (1.97) that year. Low scoring and defensive tactics are among the determinants – though not the only ones – of league positions and thus competitive balance.

AVENUES FOR FUTURE RESEARCH INCLUDING GOAL SCORING

Whatever the relationship between scoring and competitive balance, it is game attendances and TV audiences that really matter to European football leagues and clubs, since they represent the great bulk of their revenues and finance their investment in talent.

Table 8.5 Average game attendance, five major European leagues

Season	2003	2004	2005	2006	2007	Average
French *Ligue 1*	19844	20179	21325	21556	21949	20971
English Premier League	35464	35020	33890	33864	34363	34520
German *Bundesliga*	33795	37479	37786	40735	39980	37991
Italian *Lega Calcio*	25474	25474	25473	21698	17533	23130
Spanish *Liga de Futbol*	28593	28823	28402	28759	28838	28683

Source: Authors' calculation from league data.

Research is needed to check whether goal scoring has a significant influence on attendances and TV audiences.[8] A first expectation is that the lowest goal scoring league would attract the smallest attendance whereas the highest scoring league should attract the biggest attendance. Rough data on average game attendance per season shows that the French *Ligue 1*, with the highest percentage of 0–0 and 1–0 results, has the smallest attendance (Table 8.5) while the German *Bundesliga*, with the lowest percentage of low scores, attracts the biggest attendance. The English Premier League is ranked second on both indexes. The *Bundesliga*, with the highest average number of goals per game and the highest percentage of games with more than four goals, is the most attractive to fans. *Ligue 1* is the least attractive, with the lowest average number of goals per game and the lowest percentage of games with more than four goals.

In Table 8.6, average game attendance is regressed on goal scoring variables. Game attendance decreases in European football leagues with an increasing percentage of 0–0 scores. No-goal outcomes are probably boring to fans. Attendances fall with an increasing proportion of one-goal maximum games. On the other hand, attendances increase with the proportion of games with more than four goals. Fans attend to see goals; scoring probably matters in their utility function. Thus, with the same caveat as for competitive balance, a simple regression of game attendance on variables representative of goal scoring and defensive tactics suggests that attendance is related to goal scoring. However, this is only a preliminary conclusion since fan attendance is also influenced by several omitted variables that

Table 8.6   *Regression of average game attendance on goal scoring*
               variables, 2003–2007

Game attendance regressed on:	Coefficient	Constant	R2	*P* > | *t* |
Percentage of 0–0 scores	−97.248	2404.15	0.4227	0.000***
Percentage of Max. 1 goal	−52.583	3003.73	0.4888	0.000***
Percentage of > 4 goals	34.014	856.09	0.2974	0.005***
Average number of goals	1218.54	−1576.71	0.5140	0.000***

Note: *** Significant at a 1% threshold.

Source: Data from *Bundesliga, Lega Calcio, Liga de Futbol, Ligue 1* and Premier League.

we have surveyed above (section 1): the quality of the contest, the players selected, the degree of contention, the price of admission and fans' income, travel costs, availability of substitutes such as TV broadcasts, quality of viewing (quality of seating, stadium size), parking availability, timing, home advantage, supply capacity and some macroeconomic variables. However, this points to an agenda for future research which should introduce goal scoring variables in estimating the demand functions of fan attendance.

The finding that the more balanced French *Ligue 1* does not attract bigger attendances than other major European football leagues is at odds with predictions of the standard theory of team sport leagues (Fort and Quirk, 1995; Vrooman, 1995) even when it is adapted to open leagues with win-maximising clubs (Késenne, 1996, 2000b). Minimising losses on the pitch is rational economic behaviour for preventing the most disastrous consequence, that is, relegation or non-promotion of a club (Dessus and Raballand, 2009). Since major European football leagues are now dominated by four or five clubs in revenue terms and in sporting success and Champions League qualification (Andreff and Bourg, 2006; Raballand *et al.*, 2008), loss-minimising strategies are likely to spread widely throughout those clubs which have no chance of winning national championships. The rationale which is consistent with observed low scoring and defensive tactics is not win-maximising but loss-minimising[9] for most European clubs. This also opens new avenues for research into the theory of professional team leagues.

FOOTBALL ATTRACTIVENESS: COMPETITIVE BALANCE VERSUS GOAL SCORING STRATEGIES

A French government report looks at the weaknesses of professional football in France (Besson, 2008). It does not address issues such as low scoring and defensive tactics. Low attendance and TV audience are primarily attributed to the small size of French cities, limited stadium capacity and overall lack of interest in football in France. The report makes a number of economic and fiscal, but very few sporting recommendations. One is to reduce the number of clubs in *Ligue 1* from 20 to 18; another is to restrict the number of relegated teams to two instead of three. None of the recommendations tackles the issue of how to reduce the number of boring games as one of the levers for attracting more fans to more attractive games. However, decision making over the rules of the game is not within European governments' control, but is in the hands of international football's governing bodies.

With unchanged rules, any national football league can have only two basic strategies. One is to let post-Bosman free market forces deepen financial disparities between teams, which, in turn, fuels competitive balance decline and repeatedly favours the same few dominant teams. The other option is to let the defensive tactics and low scoring adopted by teams act as a countervailing force against competitive balance decline: this is the English–Italian and, to a lesser extent, Spanish solution. Here the hope is that those fans 'saved' by a slower competitive balance decline will not be 'lost' in the long run due to an increasing number of boring games. An alternative strategy is to target a better competitive balance through league regulation, including redistribution of TV rights revenues that compensates for clubs' financial disparities as a source of unbalanced contest: this is the French solution. The price paid for a good competitive balance in national championships is twofold: leading teams in a balanced league are not strong enough to win European contests (Andreff and Bourg, 2006) while defensive tactics and low scoring offset the benefits of good competitive balance.

In both strategies, there is a trade-off between attracting attendance with competitive balance and scoring attractiveness, since competitive balance improves with growing 0–0 and 1–0 scores. Of the five major European leagues, only the *Bundesliga* seems to have circumvented this trade-off, combining the best goal scoring performance with a quite good competitive balance – a mix which appears to have been successful in attracting fans. Consequently, we conclude with a plea for rules that provide goal scoring incentives so that the share of 0–0 and 1–0 results will diminish, the number of goals scored will increase, and the attractiveness of the game to fans will be enhanced.

ACKNOWLEDGEMENTS

The authors thank Madeleine Andreff and Boris Najman for methodological suggestions provided on a first draft of this chapter and Alan Whitworth for editing and comments and suggestions.

NOTES

1. We assume that there is no match fixing and no rigged games even though this is a serious issue in current international football (Hill, 2009). Corruption in Italian football is so significant that it has recently drawn the attention of 'non-sport economists' like Boeri and Severgnini (2009).
2. Groot elaborates on alternative and more sophisticated statistical measures of competitive balance (the surprise index and the team quality index), but without breaking the established link with goal scoring.
3. Two other variables impact on competitive balance in Groot's approach: imperfect or erratic referees and home and away (dis)advantage.
4. The same percentage was seen during the 1998 World Cup.
5. Since both Groot (2008) and Raballand *et al.* (2008) assert a link – without testing it so far – between the model of professional sport finance, goal scoring and competitive balance, further research should scrutinise the potential role of sport finance as a determinant of goal scoring and competitive balance.
6. Both 1–0 (home field) and 0–1 (away) are counted together; we do not test home advantage here.
7. According to the Breusch-Pagan test, it is not necessary to take random effects into account ($Pr > Chi2 = 0.85$); thus we retain the OLS estimation of equation (8.3) in Table 8.4.
8. A paper by Alavy *et al.* (2010) on TV audiences for English Premier League football from January 2003 to May 2005 shows that a no-score draw does not attract as many TV viewers as a 0–1 or 1–0 result.
9. Although, in mathematical terms, win maximising and loss minimising will lead to the same formal equilibrium solution in the theoretical standard model of a professional team sports league, the empirical consequences on the pitch in terms of goal scoring and, presumably, at the gate in terms of attendance must be different.

REFERENCES

Alavy, K., Gaskell, A., Leach, S. and Szymanski, S. (2010), 'On the Edge of Your Seat: Demand for Football on Television and the Uncertainty of Outcome Hypothesis', *International Journal of Sport Finance*, 5(2), 75–95.

Amann, E., Dewenter, R. and Namini, J.E. (2004), *The Home-Bias Paradox in Football*, discussion paper, Essen: University of Duisburg-Essen.

Andreff, W. (1981), 'Le prix du spectacle sportif et le comportement du spectateur', in *Le spectacle sportif*, Paris: Presses Universitaires de France, 60–83.

Andreff, W. (2009), 'Equilibre compétitif et contrainte budgétaire dans une ligue de sport professionnel', *Revue Economique*, 60, 591–633.

Andreff, W. and Bourg, J.-F. (2006), 'Broadcasting Rights and Competition in European Football', in C. Jeanrenaud and S. Késenne (eds), *The Economics of Sport and the Media*, Cheltenham: Edward Elgar, 37–70.

Andreff, W. and Nys, J.-F. (1986), *Economie du sport*, Que sais-je? no. 2294, Paris: Presses Universitaires de France.

Andreff, W. and Staudohar, P. (2000), 'The Evolving European Model of Professional Sports Finance', *Journal of Sports Economics*, 1, 257–76.

Avrillier, R. (1978), 'Note de discussion sur l'histoire du football', *Séminaire Socio-économie du sport*, University of Grenoble 2, February, mimeo.

Aylott, M. and Aylott, N. (2007), 'A Meeting of Social Science and Football: Measuring the Effects of Three Points for a Win', *Sports in Science*, 10, 205–22.

Baimbridge, M., Cameron, S. and Dawson, P. (1996), 'Satellite Television and the Demand for Football: A Whole New Ball Game?' *Scottish Journal of Political Economy*, 43, 317–33.

Besson, E. (2008), *Accroître la compétitivité des clubs de football professionnel français*, Rapport au Premier Ministre du Secrétariat d'Etat chargé de la Prospective, de l'Evaluation des Politiques Publiques et du Développement de l'Economie Numérique, Paris.

Bird, P.J.W.N. (1982), 'The Demand for League Football', *Applied Economics*, 14, 637–49.

Boeri, T. and Severgnini, B. (2009), *The Italian Job: Match Rigging, Career Concern and Media Concentration in Serie A*, Milan: Bocconi University, mimeo.

Borland, J. (1987), 'The Demand for Australian Rules Football', *Economic Record*, 63, 220–30.

Borland, J. and Macdonald, R. (2003), 'Demand for Sport', *Oxford Review of Economic Policy*, 19, 478–502.

Brocas, I. and Carrillo, J.D. (2004), 'Do the "Three-Point Victory" and "Golden Goal" Rules Make Soccer More Exciting? A Theoretical Analysis of a Simple Game', *Journal of Sports Economics*, 5, 169–85.

Cairns, J. (1987), 'Evaluating Changes in League Structure: The Reorganisation of the Scottish Football League', *Applied Economics*, 19, 259–75.

Davies, B., Downward, P. and Jackson, I. (1995), 'The Demand for Rugby League: Evidence from Causality Tests', *Applied Economics*, 27, 1003–07.

Dessus, S. and Raballand, G. (2009), *Budgets optimaux et compétitivité des clubs de football français*, Washington, mimeo.

Dilger, A. and Geyer, H. (2009), 'Are Three Points for a Win Really Better Than Two? A Comparison of German Soccer League and Cup Games', *Journal of Sports Economics*, 10, 305–17.

Dobson, S. and Goddard, J. (1992), 'The Demand for Standing and Seated Viewing Accommodation in the English Football League', *Applied Economics*, 24, 1155–63.

Dobson, S. and Goddard, J. (1995), 'The Demand for Professional League Football in England and Wales, 1925–92', *The Statistician*, 44 (2), 259–77.

El-Hodiri, M. and Quirk, J. (1971), 'An Economic Model of a Professional Sports League', *Journal of Political Economy*, 79, 1302–19.

Forrest, D. and Simmons, R. (2002), 'Outcome Uncertainty and Attendance in Sport: The Case of English Soccer', *The Statistician*, 51, 229–41.

Forrest, D., Simmons, R. and Feehan, P. (2002), 'A Spatial Cross-sectional Analysis of the Elasticity of Demand for Soccer', *Scottish Journal of Political Economy*, 49, 336–55.

Fort, R. and Quirk, J. (1995), 'Cross-subsidization, Incentives, and Outcomes in Professional Team Leagues', *Journal of Economic Literature*, 33, 1265–99.

Garicano, L. and Palacios-Huerta, I. (2006), *Sabotage in Tournaments: Making the Beautiful Game a Bit Less Beautiful*, Research paper, Brown University, Providence, RI.

Gerrard, B. (2006), 'Analysing the Win–Wage Relationship in Pro Sports Leagues: Evidence from the FA Premier League, 1997/98 to 2001/02', in P. Rodriguez, S. Késenne and J. Garcia (eds), *Sports Economics after Fifty Years: Essays in Honour of Simon Rottenberg*, Oviedo: Ediciones de la Universidad de Oviedo, 169–90.

Groot, L. (2008), *Economics, Uncertainty and European Football: Trends in Competitive Balance*, Cheltenham: Edward Elgar.

Guedes, J.C. and Machado, F.S. (2002), 'Changing Rewards in Contests: Has the Three-Point-Rule Brought more Offense to Soccer?' *Empirical Economics*, 27, 607–30.

Hall, S., Szymanski, S. and Zimbalist, A. (2002), 'Testing Causality between Team Performance and Payroll: The Cases of Major League Baseball and English Soccer', *Journal of Sports Economics*, 3, 149–68.

Hill, D. (2009), 'How Gambling Corruptors Fix Football Matches', *European Sport Management Quarterly*, 9, 411–32.

Hoehn, T. and Szymanski, S. (1999), 'The Americanization of European Football', *Economic Policy*, 28, 205–33.

Hundsdoerfer, J. (2004), 'Fördert die 3-Punkte-Regel den offensiven Fussball?' in P. Hammann, L. Schmidt and M. Welling (eds), *Ökonomie des Fussballs: Grundlegungen aus volks- und betriebswirtschaftlicher Perspektive*, Wiesbaden: Deutscher Universitäts-Verlag.

Jennett, N. (1984), 'Attendances, Uncertainty of Outcome and Policy in

Scottish League Football', *Scottish Journal of Political Economy*, 31, 176–98.

Késenne, S. (1996), 'League Management in Professional Team Sports within Win Maximizing Clubs', *European Journal of Sport Management*, 2, 14–22.

Késenne, S. (2000a), 'The Impact of Salary Caps in Professional Team Sports', *Scottish Journal of Political Economy*, 47, 431–55.

Késenne, S. (2000b), 'Revenue Sharing and Competitive Balance in Professional Team Sports', *Journal of Sports Economics*, 1, 56–65.

McDonald, M. and Rascher, D. (2000), 'Does Bat Day Make Cents? The Effect of Promotions on the Demand for Major League Baseball', *Journal of Sport Management*, 14, 8–27.

Neale, W.C. (1964), 'The Peculiar Economics of Professional Sports: A Contribution to the Theory of the Firm in Sporting Competition and in Market Competition', *Quarterly Journal of Economics*, 78, 1–14.

Peel, D. and Thomas, D. (1992), 'The Demand for Football: Some Evidence of Outcome Uncertainty', *Empirical Economics*, 17, 323–31.

Raballand, G., Cianferani, S. and Marteau, J.-F. (2008), *Quel avenir pour le football? Objectif 0–0*, Paris: L'Harmattan.

Scully, G. (1995), *The Market Structure of Sports*, Chicago: The University of Chicago Press.

Shepotylo, O. (2006), 'Three-Point-for-Win in Soccer Rule: Are there Incentives for Match Fixing?' in O. Shepotylo, *Three Essays on Institutions and Economic Development*, PhD dissertation, University of Maryland, College Park.

Simmons, R. (1996), 'The Demand for English League Football: A Club-Level Analysis', *Applied Economics*, 28, 139–55.

Sloane, P. (1971), 'The Economics of Professional Football: The Football Club as a Utility Maximiser', *Scottish Journal of Political Economy*, 18, 121–46.

Szymanski, S. (2001), 'Income Inequality, Competitive Balance and the Attractiveness of Team Sports: Some Evidence and a Natural Experiment from English Soccer', *Economic Journal*, 111, F69–84.

Szymanski, S. (2003), 'The Economic Design of Sporting Contests', *Journal of Economic Literature*, 61, 1137–87.

Szymanski, S. (2004), 'Professional Team Sports are only a Game: The Walrasian Fixed-Supply Model, Contest-Nash Equilibrium, and the Invariance Principle', *Journal of Sports Economics*, 5, 111–26.

Szymanski, S. and Késenne, S. (2004), 'Competitive Balance and Gate Revenue Sharing in Team Sports', *Journal of Industrial Economics*, 51, 513–25.

Szymanski, S. and Kuypers, T. (1999), *Winners and Losers: The Business Strategy of Football*, London: Viking.

Vrooman, J. (1995), 'A General Theory of Professional Sports Leagues', *Southern Economic Journal*, 61, 971–90.

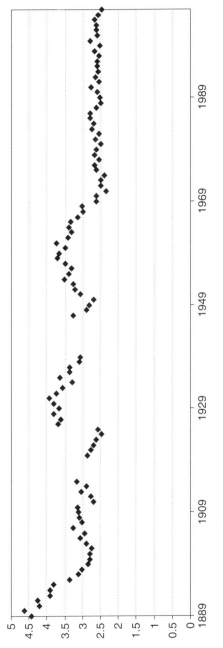

Figure 8A.1a   English Premier League goal averages

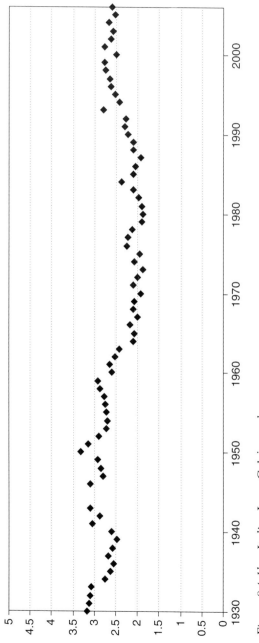

Figure 8A.1b   Italian Lega Calcio goal averages

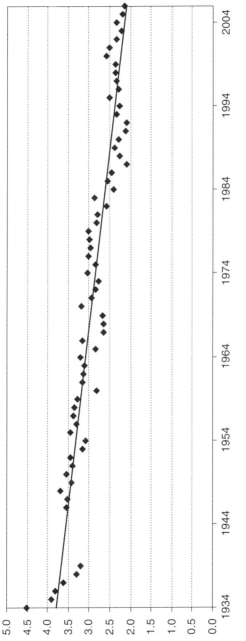

Figure 8A.1c   French Ligue 1 goal averages

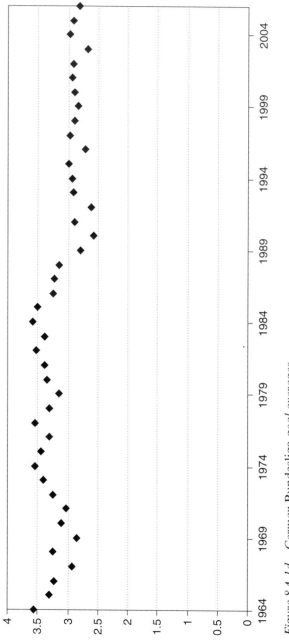

Figure 8A.1d German Bundesliga goal averages

APPENDIX B: LEAGUE COMPETITIVE BALANCE AND GOAL SCORING

Table 8B.3a   Competitive balance and goal scoring, French Ligue 1

Season	2003	2004	2005	2006	2007	Average
Competitive balance*	1.28	1.46	1.10	1.44	1.06	1.27
A = % of 0–0scores/ all scores	**12.4**	**9.5**	**14.2**	**13.4**	**12.9**	**12.5**
B = % of 1–0 scores/ all scores	25.5	21.8	21.6	23.7	21.3	22.8
C = % of games with max.1 goal	*37.9*	*31.3*	*35.8*	*37.1*	*34.2*	*35.3*
D = % of games with > 4 goals	11.1	12.1	7.9	13.7	5.8	10.1
E = D/C = attractive- ness ratio	0.29	0.39	0.22	0.37	0.17	0.29
Number of goals per game	2.20	2.33	2.17	2.13	2.25	2.22

Table 8B.3b   Competitive balance and goal scoring, German Bundesliga

Season	2003	2004	2005	2006	2007	Average
Competitive balance*	1.23	1.61	1.50	1.53	1.30	1.27
A = % of 0–0 scores/ all scores	**6.5**	**6.2**	**5.9**	**7.8**	**7.8**	**6.9**
B = % of 1–0 scores/ all scores	18.0	15.7	14.0	13.4	14.7	15.2
C = % of games with max.1 goal	*24.5*	*21.9*	*19.9*	*21.2*	*22.5*	*22.0*
D = % of games with > 4 goals	22.2	25.5	26.5	20.9	23.9	23.8
E = D/C = attractive- ness ratio	0.91	1.16	1.33	0.98	1.06	1.08
Number of goals per game	2.68	2.97	2.91	2.81	2.74	2.82

Table 8B.3c   *Competitive balance and goal scoring, Spanish* Liga de
            Futbol

Season	2003	2004	2005	2006	2007	Average
Competitive balance*	1.32	1.28	1.51	1.49	1.39	1.40
A = % of 0–0 scores/ all scores	**8.4**	**5.3**	**7.6**	**7.1**	**10.0**	**7.7**
B = % of 1–0 scores/ all scores	19.0	19.4	19.2	19.2	20.5	19.5
C = % of games with max. 1 goal	*27.4*	*24.7*	*26.8*	*26.3*	*30.5*	*27.2*
D = % of games with > 4 goals	23.7	21.6	21.8	17.6	25.5	22.1
E = D/C = attractiveness ratio	0.87	0.87	0.81	0.67	0.84	0.81
Number of goals per game	2.67	2.67	2.58	2.46	2.48	2.57

Table 8B.3d   *Competitive balance and goal scoring, English Premier
            League*

Season	2003	2004	2005	2006	2007	Average
Competitive balance*	1.62	1.57	1.73	1.94	1.64	1.70
A = % of 0–0 scores/ all scores	**5.5**	**10.8**	**7.9**	**8.4**	**8.9**	**8.3**
B = % of 1–0 scores/ all scores	21.3	16.3	20.8	21.6	19.8	20.0
C = % of games with max. 1 goal	*26.8*	*27.1*	*28.7*	*30.0*	*28.7*	*28.3*
D = % of games with > 4 goals	19.7	23.9	21.8	17.1	23.4	21.2
E = D/C = attractiveness ratio	0.74	0.88	0.76	0.57	0.82	0.75
Number of goals per game	2.63	2.66	2.57	2.48	2.45	2.56

Table 8B.3e   *Competitive balance and goal scoring, Italian* Lega
Calcio

Season	2003	2004	2005	2006	2007	Average
Competitive balance*	1.56	1.86	1.45	1.97	1.78	1.72
A = % of 0–0 scores/	**9.2**	**10.5**	**9.5**	**8.2**	**10.3**	**9.5**
all scores						
B = % of 1–0 scores/	16.0	14.7	22.3	15.7	20.0	17.7
all scores						
C = % of games with	*25.2*	*25.2*	*31.8*	*23.9*	*30.3*	*27.3*
max. 1 goal						
D = % of games with	19.3	29.4	17.9	22.1	22.4	22.2
> 4 goals						
E = D/C = attractive-	0.77	1.17	0.56	0.92	0.74	0.81
ness ratio						
Number of goals per	2.58	2.67	2.53	2.61	2.55	2.59
game						

Note: * Noll-Scully index, 5 league average (from Table 8.1).

Source: Authors' calculation from league data.

Index